Politics, Policy
and
Nursing

*To Derek, Gareth and Brendan
with my love*

Politics, Policy and Nursing

Anita Fatchett

MA, BA(Hons), RHV, RN, Cert.Ed.
Senior Lecturer in Nursing
Leeds Metropolitan University
Leeds, UK

Baillière Tindall
London   Philadelphia   Toronto   Sydney   Tokyo

Baillière Tindall   24–28 Oval Road
W. B. Saunders   London NW1 7DX

The Curtis Center
Independence Square West
Philadelphia, PA 19106-3399, USA

Harcourt Brace & Company
55 Horner Avenue
Toronto, Ontario, M8Z 4X6, Canada

Harcourt Brace & Company, Australia
30–52 Smidmore Street
Marrickville
NSW 2204, Australia

Harcourt Brace & Company, Japan
Ichibancho Central Building
21–1 Ichibancho
Chiyoda-ku, Tokyo 102, Japan

A catalogue record for this book is available from the British Library

ISBN 0-7020-1791 4

Typeset by Phoenix Photosetting, Lordswood, Chatham, Kent
Printed and bound in Great Britain by
Mackays of Chatham PLC, Chatham, Kent

Contents

Foreword

The NHS ranks as one of the most successful innovations in social policy of the century. It represents a brave assertion of the equal value of human life by ensuring that patients get the treatment they need rather than the treatment they can afford. Moreover, because the NHS provides no financial incentive to treatment that patients do not need, it has contained rising medical costs more successfully than market driven medical systems such as the US models.

It has of course its own fair share of warts. In my period as Health Spokesman I came to be particularly concerned over two strategic failings. Firstly, I fully shared the impatience of the present author with the low priority attached to prevention rather than treatment of disease. Secondly, I was frustrated by the extent to which the glamour and prestige of dramatic surgery distracted attention and resources from the more socially useful application of healthcare to chronic conditions.

However, the recent upheaval in the NHS was not motivated by any concern over its failings, but by resentment at its very success. I believe it was precisely because of its success in providing a popular and efficient alternative to market solutions that Mrs Thatcher maintained a manifest and deep hostility to the NHS. The 'Reforms' over which she presided in her final years should not be seen as an isolated response to a specific funding crisis, but as a deliberate attempt to remould the human centred values of a public service into the commercially driven values of the market economy.

The most objectionable feature of the changes is their dehumanising culture. Patient need is no longer the motor force of the system. In the new pseudo-market, patients are not the clients but the units of exchange in which managers conduct their 'purchasing' agreements.

Part of the ideological prejudice behind the Reforms was a thinly veiled contempt for any concept of professional ethics. Politicians who understand only market solutions are unlikely to comprehend or respect staff motivation that is not an opportunistic response to a commercial opening. The danger is that the result will be to squeeze out of the NHS the dedication and commitment of health workers which has repeatedly compensated for chronic lack of resources.

Anita Fatchett has provided a timely analysis of the challenge which the new commercial culture poses to both health staff and patients. This study supplies a sober assessment of the impact of the Reforms on patient care and a unique commentary on how they are changing the role of the nursing profession. She has made a valuable contribution to the debate on the present state of the NHS and on its future direction.

Nurses supply half the staffing of the NHS and most of its patient contact. Their perspective on the Health Service is a useful corrective to the managerial agenda of the establishment. This book should be made available on prescription to every director of an NHS Trust.

Robin Cook M.P.
July 1994

1

Introduction

Thanks to the National Health Service the population of the United Kingdom has been entitled to health care free at the point of need for over forty years. The NHS is something of which we can be justifiably proud in this country, reflecting, as it does, a society expressing a practical concern for the health and well-being of all its members. In spite of its many faults, it has been described as the envy of the world, and other countries – even today – are seeking to adopt its values and emulate its systems. Sadly, and perhaps surprisingly, it appears that its continuation as a great British public institution is under threat.

This service which is paid for by taxation, which has been relatively efficient, and which over time has attempted to achieve some sort of equitable distribution of health care, now appears to be in the middle of the process of being changed into a fragmented and marketized national health care provider, too often starved of necessary resources. Those nurses educated and trained within the NHS, and who promote and reflect its essential values, surely now have good reason to be concerned about its future health and well-being.

This book is about developing that general concern for the survival of the NHS into a more informed response from nurses. It follows the path of earlier writers on politics and nursing like Salvage who, in 1985, encouraged nurses to challenge the adverse consequences of political and policy decisions as they affected them in their work and in their personal experiences of those decisions at the bedside. Clay, in similar vein in 1987, encouraged nurses to look beyond the immediate frustration of not being able to give all they would wish to their patients. He asked them to do all in their power to ensure that future generations gained the nurses and the nursing care which they deserved. This book then, updates and carries on their themes, and looks at nursing in the newly reforming NHS as it makes its way to the twenty-first century.

The central focus of all the subsequent discussions is that of the new style NHS which has been slowly emerging over the past decade or so. It will highlight the apparent rebirth of the discredited market approach to health care distribution of the past. That old system in pre-NHS times proved to be a failure because of its obvious unfairness for large, poorer groups in the population who could not afford to buy all the health care they needed. In present day, recession hit 1990s Britain, it is surely questionable whether the old ways will meet with greater success a second time around. As we will be reminded, the creation of the NHS in the late 1940s was a collective response, initiated by the then Labour Government, to meet the health care needs of all the population. It reflected a clear acknowledgement that the previous market arrangements in health care provision had failed to rise to the task, and that good health and access to health care should not depend on any one person's spending ability, but should be something which everyone is entitled to enjoy within a developed society.

It is plain then, that all nurses have a vested interest in being involved in any discussions around such issues, not just because they work in the NHS and are naturally concerned for their own futures within it, but because they and their families as tax-payers, as users of the health services and as voters, have an interest, too. The re-election of the

Conservative Government for a fourth term of office in April 1992 signalled 'full steam ahead' for the continuation of the redesigning and repackaging of the NHS which has been underway for well over a decade.

Nurses are only too aware of just how difficult this period of recent internal change has been for them. They have endured the impacts of major political and managerial change within the NHS. Increasingly they have found themselves working within a commercialized and fragmented organization, and feeling the impact of shortages and strict rationing of resources. This has certainly not been an easy time, particularly for those in face-to-face contact with patients. Sadly, the specific promise to consumers of more power and choice of care has not necessarily been matched with the means to meet the ever-rising demands. In one sense nurses appear to have been made 'the piggy in the middle' and in many instances asked to do the impossible. Whilst the NHS Management Executive (Department of Health, 1993) sets out what it described as 'an ambitious strategy' for nursing, and reminds us that 'improving health and making care services better is heavily dependent upon nurses, midwives and health visitors', at the same time the credibility of nursing as a profession is clearly in doubt and under attack. Like many of the disappointed consumers in the health service, it might also be argued that nurses are being let down by the Government. It is clearly time to try and develop some understanding of the combination of forces which has led to the situation that nurses now find themselves in. A failure to respond to the changes could well result in a failure to survive as a profession.

In Chapters 2 to 5 the aim is to help nurses clarify what appears to be going on around them. The author will try to examine some aspects of the reforms from a nurse's point of view. The chapters will consider the historical background and political reasoning behind the changes. They will remind the reader of why we have an NHS and look to what has happened to it over time, and specifically, of course, in recent times.

As we will see, the NHS reforms are just one part of the wider political plans of the Government for all public spending areas. Financial retrenchment has not only had an impact on the contextual settings of nurse caring but, inevitably, its knock-on effects have made impressions on the content of that care. In these ways it will be argued that outside political forces appear to be both controlling and shaping developments within the nursing profession and not necessarily, it will be suggested, for the better. Hopefully, the discussions will help to develop the will to create strategies to redirect our steps for ourselves, and to avoid being pushed into a shape created by others who appear to neither support an NHS nor understand the role of nurses.

The chapters to follow, therefore, will examine four particular areas of interest for all nurses.

Chapter 2   The creation of the internal health care market and its impact on the NHS as an organization for distributing health care to all of the population.

In this chapter, claims about the beneficial impact of the creation and workings of the internal health care market, although relatively new, will be shown to be open to question. Arguments as to the success of the changes are countered by those who beg to differ. It is clearly debatable whether or not nurses have been enabled to give better care as promised. Concerns as to the alleged underfunding of the services and to its consequent impact on services available to consumers will challenge the veracity of promises of

greater consumer power and choice within the new purchaser–provider relationships.

Chapter 3   The redefinition of the patients/clients of the NHS as consumers in the new commercial-type relationships created by the reforms.

Moving on to Chapter 3 we will think about the consumers
of the health services. Consideration will be given to the
intention of strengthening the users' position in the NHS by
virtue of the reforms. Again, whilst some will be in no
doubt as to progress made in this area, others will disagree.
They will claim that the changes are not about increasing
choice and listening more to the consumers, but rather a
well-packaged ploy to cover up cost containment and a
slow dismantling of the broadly based care remit of a
national care service.

Chapter 4   The intention of the NHS to remain the major health promoter of the nation.

Chapter 4 looks to the future potential role of the NHS as a
major health promoter. Evidence presented will cast doubts
on the intention of the Government to lead the NHS into
providing a coherent and effective health promotion strategy – in spite of apparent promises to the contrary in the
White Paper *The Health of the Nation* (Department of
Health, 1992). Rather, the service will be presented as on
the road to an even more limited medicalized framework
for care than ever before. Within this, the potential for nurse
role developments in the wider environmental and social
health fields looks worryingly questionable. Indeed, it will
be suggested that the extent of any new agenda for the NHS

is likely to be constrained because of the continuing down-ward pressure on all public spending. As a result, any real financial or political backing for nurse role development in wider health promotional fields looks doubtful, and will create some disappointment for the many nurses who aspire to greater positive health care opportunities within their work.

Chapter 5   The challenges of the reforms to the development of nursing as a profession.

In Chapter 5 we will turn to nursing and professional devel-opment issues; considering nurse fears and concerns for nursing and its likely future. We note that the professional credibility being sought by nurses appears to be slow in coming, judging from, for example, recent treatment of nurses by the Government in pay awards. Challenges to nurse values, code of practice and autonomy are apparent from the increasing controls being placed on what they as NHS employees might wish to say about the negative impacts of the reforms on patient care and standards. Others, who support the Government's approach to health care, appear to be orchestrating nurse developments from outside the profession. Trends might suggest the potential creation of a two-tier nursing body in the future.

In all chapters the outcomes of the changes made will be questioned, both for the NHS as a major national health care provider organization, and also for the nursing profes-sion and its future. Whilst the conclusions reflect a number of very worrying concerns, the common theme is one of a fear for the durability of collective security of the NHS both for us as nurses and as users.

In essence then, as in previous books concerned with nurs-ing and politics, nurses are again being confronted by the often uncomfortable realities of their working lives. They are being challenged to think about these realities in relation to the survival of a nursing profession as they would like it to be. The concluding chapter will look to discussing some potential future strategies and to encourage like others before a collective nurse response.

My conclusions might prove not always to be accepted or acceptable. Others might be more sanguine about the NHS and nursing. They may feel all is well. Disagreement following debate, however, is not a bad thing: no debate, and implied unthinking acquiescence, are the real causes of concern. If this book stimulates a better informed debate, it will most certainly have served its purpose.

References

Clay Trevor (1987) *Nurses, Power and Politics*. London, Heinemann.

Department of Health (1992) *The Health of the Nation*. London, HMSO.

Department of Health (1993) *A Vision For The Future*. NHS Management Executive. London, DOH.

Salvage Jane (1985) *Politics Of Nursing*. London, Heinemann.

2

The NHS and the Internal Health Care Market

'The Government will build further on the strengths of the NHS, whilst tackling its weaknesses. This will ensure that the NHS becomes an even stronger, more modern service, more committed than ever to working for patients.' (Department of Health, 1989a). The method chosen for delivering this promise has been the creation of an internal health care market, and the application of the financial disciplines of the commercial sector. The introduction of the NHS market on 1 April 1991 represented a profound change of direction in the way in which health care was to be distributed in the UK. The implications of NHS market developments over time are likely to change the shape, size and philosophy of NHS practice for both those who use its services and for those who work within it.

However, proponents of the proposed changes promised that all would be well. As Clarke (then Secretary of State for Health) said:

Taken together, these proposals add up to the most formidable programme of reform in the history of the NHS. They are the latest step in our drive to build a stronger, more modern, more efficient health service. An NHS that is run better will be an NHS that can care better . . . I trust that all those who – like me – truly believe in a Health Service that offers a high quality care to all our people will lend their support to these reforms (Clarke, 1989a).

Political opponents of the proposals were appalled. Cook (Labour Shadow Health Secretary) in the same debate described the proposed changes as:

The prescription for a Health Service run by accountants for Civil Servants, written by people who will always put a healthy balance sheet before healthy patients . . . The White Paper is the product of a review behind closed doors by closed minds. Junior ministers, we read, were consulted over dinner at No. 10. Junior doctors were not consulted. Nurses were not consulted. Patients were not consulted. The result is a series of proposals that will be unworkable as they will be unpopular (Cook, 1989).

This chapter will look to the review, the list of alleged NHS failures, and the Conservative Government's response to these with particular reference to the internal market solution. Issues surrounding the notion of a market in health care will be discussed and readers will be encouraged to reflect on these examples in light of their experiences so far in the new style NHS.

Two questions will provide an appropriate framework:

1 What are the implications of the creation of an internal health care market for the NHS and its future?
2 Are nurses going to be able to give higher standards of care promised as a result of the market changes?

Some answers to these questions are vital for nurses and their future practice. The changes are evolving at a great pace. For some, this means that the agenda of nurses 'remains packed'. As one editor put it:

The main priority must be the survival of nursing values and expertise in a climate where many of the people who control services politically or managerially seem to know the cost of everything and the value of nothing. More than ever it is vital that nurses seek to explain and demonstrate to politicians of every hue the contribution of the profession to patients' care (Editorial, *Nursing Times*, 1992).

Background to the review of the NHS

Reviewing and reforming health care institutions is not a peculiarly late twentieth century British pastime. Other countries are also expressing dissatisfaction with their own systems of health care delivery and finance and, like us, they are searching for some better way. We only need to look to western Europe to find countries such as Germany, France and The Netherlands looking to solve their particular problems. Across the Atlantic also, many Americans, including the public, health professionals, economists and politicians alike are presently expressing doubt at their health care system. They are losing faith in their market-led services which they perceive as failing, and are looking towards the creation and imposition of a more equitable, less costly, more comprehensive system of health provision for the US population. Indeed, the Clinton administration's health team, headed by Hillary Clinton, is presently working on overhauling US domestic health policy. The effort to cut and control the astronomical costs of care, to relieve the extreme pressure on state schemes of health provision, and to address the disgrace of many millions of people receiving no health cover at all, is involving a worldwide search for solutions – including the publicly-funded UK model.

It may seem strange then, that we who have based our health care services on central planning by government, and paid for by public expenditure, are now looking to market competition like in the United States as a means of controlling costs, improving our efficiency, and becoming more consumer orientated. This could well be described as a case of not learning from others' bad experiences or, indeed, not even looking back on our own pre-NHS history of health care. The failure of those times to develop adequate health care provision for all, regardless of personal income, provided without doubt the impetus for the creation of the National Health Service in 1948. Harman (Labour Health spokesperson) referred to this collective amnesia when she commented that:

> Perhaps after nearly half a century of the NHS we have forgotten the fear of financial ruin that illness can bring. We have no fear that the operation the doctor is suggesting is for the benefit of his finances rather than our health. In the US over-treatment is endemic. Yet the Government is pushing us towards an American style health care system by a combination of under-funding the NHS, subjecting it to commercial pressures and creeping privatisation (Harman, 1991b).

Many nurses, along with other commentators, understand the potential threat of damage to the health and well-being of the NHS, by relying upon any model of health care which has failed both elsewhere and previously. Benner, for example, has expressed astonishment at such a solution for NHS problems. She refers supportively to the NHS as 'the most inclusive health care system', 'the most economical health care system', and 'the envy of the USA' (Benner, 1991).

We may well then ask, how did we arrive at a prescription to cure the alleged ills of the old-style NHS which, according to many commentators, may well lead to an American type of health care distribution and finance with many of its apparent faults? Are we now part of a move towards mass privatization, increased commercialization, and a two-tiered health service which may well serve a minority well but only at the expense of a large majority who could, it is argued, end up with little or no health care at all. We will have to cast our minds back a little to begin to understand the answer.

How it happened – a background to the NHS reforms

Firstly, we need to reflect briefly on the historical background to the NHS, noting that it was formed to deal with the social inequalities of a largely market-driven health care system. Secondly, some consideration will be given to why and how the post-war consensus of support for the NHS started to weaken in the early 1970s. Thirdly, we will see how the NHS Review appeared to be bounced onto the health policy agenda by Margaret Thatcher during a television programme in January 1988. That sudden announcement should be etched on our minds, like other significant political events, because of the implications for all who support a national health service.

Historical background to the discussion

The creation of a National Health Service after the Second World War represented the rejection of the market-based provision of health care services which had developed over many decades. As with educational provision, housing and employment opportunity, it was acknowledged that individuals 'standing on their own two feet' were not always able to look after themselves or to protect themselves from those uncontrollable external factors which impinged upon their health and well-being (e.g. economic recession and unemployment, low income, pollution, dangerous working environment, and poor housing). A belief had grown that society should collectively contribute towards the provision of a major institutional social support system. Thus the welfare state came into being to equalize the potential opportunity for all citizens, and thus all consumers, to meet their health and social needs.

The values underpinning these changes reflected an acknowledgement of, and general responsibility for each member of society, collectively insuring against the personal, financial and social costs of the unexpected, ill-health and other misfortune. Health care and good health were not to be seen as some consumer product to be bought and sold in a market place, or to be dependent upon any one individual's spending power. Also, unlike when buying biscuits, no lay person knew enough about health to choose this or that care. Similarly, unlike returning and complaining about faulty shop goods, it was clearly not easy or indeed in some cases possible to trade-in or question defective care, malpractice or some irreversible life-threatening treatment. The market in health care provision had been a failure for a large part of the population. The new collectivist solution to meeting health care needs for all people, and not just for some, was exemplified by the creation of the NHS. All consumers needed to be helped to their health care, rather than trying to help themselves, and the NHS would be the vehicle.

The new National Health Service was introduced by the Labour Government in 1948, in spite of tremendous arguments against it by both Conservative politicians in opposition, and also by many in the medical profession. However, as Foot recalls in his writings about the period, Aneurin Bevan (Secretary of State for Health), on behalf of the post-war Labour Government, moved forward in what was described as 'doing the most civilised thing in the world' – putting the welfare of the sick in front of other post-war national considerations (Foot, 1973).

The rise and fall of consensus

As we have already noted, the Conservative Party opposed the introduction of the NHS. They assumed a similar approach to other legislation which helped to establish the post-war welfare state. They, however, shifted their position by the time of the 1950 General Election, realising that opposition would reduce their chances of being re-elected. Consequently the 1950s and 1960s saw a broad political consensus, often called *Butskellism*, in which the Welfare State and full employment featured as key items in the programmes of all political parties.

This consensus across the political spectrum lasted until the late 1960s when the apparent under-performance of the economy was seen by the political right as resulting from high public spending and direct taxation. Markets, individual freedom and responsibility came back into fashion, leading to the 'Selsdon Man' approach of the Conservatives under Ted Heath's leadership.

Whilst it can be argued that the Heath Government of 1970–1974 soon moved back to a consensus approach, the new right-wing thinking continued to gain ground. The failure of the Heath Government was blamed by many in the Conservative Party upon its alleged betrayal of right-wing policies. With the election of Margaret Thatcher as Conservative Party leader, a new vigour was given to the encouragement of right-wing ideas and policies. As part of what became a new hegemony the right targetted what they saw as excessive and wasteful public spending.

From the late 1970s onwards all public sector bodies including the NHS were accused by the Conservative Government of being under the dead hand of local and central public sector bureaucracies, held back by the restrictive practices of powerful professional groups, offering no real consumer choice, demonstrating indifference to quality issues, providing a lack of incentives for innovation and efficiency, and displaying a profound reliance on government funding. In addition, the NHS specifically was seen as a vast and growing consumer of public funds. Indeed it was argued, a variety of problems and challenges directly related to the NHS would, if not addressed, consume more and more of public spending, to the detriment of other important programmes.

Trends of importance causing concern

Demographic trends showed an increasing number of people living to old age and a decline in the numbers of the working population (Central Statistical Office, 1993). The subsequent proportional decrease in national insurance and tax contributions from those of working age would mean that the NHS would increasingly be limited in its ability to meet the expected health care needs of the growing elderly population.

Advances in medical knowledge and technology, including new innovations in surgery, drug therapies, advanced screening facilities and diagnostic ability, have in turn created new demands and raised the costs of the NHS in paying for the use of these facilities for its clients. In addition, to this, public expectations have risen over time as new possibilities for care have been introduced. People have become better educated and informed on health and health care matters and as such have developed as health care consumers, demanding more and more from the NHS; particularly the middle classes (Black, 1980; Whitehead 1987). So higher standards of care coupled with increased opportunity for treatment have all combined to push up NHS costs – an outcome not envisaged by Beveridge in the 1940s. He and the other creators of the NHS expected that the cost of the Health Service would fall as people's needs were met by the new services:

> With each pair of specs dispensed, each tooth stopped or set of gnashers issued, each ailment cured or chronic disease eliminated, its task and costs would be reduced. Beveridge had no conception of medical science as it really is: in a state

of dynamic expansion, always devising new health tests for new diseases, new cures and treatments, new drugs and equipment, each more expensive than the last (Welch, 1993).

The new Conservative Government of the late 1970s was clearly aware of all these trends and their long-term impact on public expenditure. Whilst providing reassurance as to the safety of the NHS in their hands, the Government started on the changes which would be necessary for the creation of a new style business-like health service, one which they felt would be better equipped to deal with the health issues and agendas of the 1980s and the 1990s.

The Government looked, it might be argued, to changes which would lead to a 'new contract between public health services and their customers, making a break with the provider-driven, paternalistic welfare approach which has been the dominant *modus operandi* in health and social care since the Second World War.' (Hunter, 1993).

Across all welfare institutions, including health, the Government began to push back the remits of state provision both by slowing down and reversing the growth in public spending. Some public services were part or wholly privatized following the introduction of competitive tendering in 1983 (Gaze, 1990; Laurent, 1990). Increasing use was being made of information technology both to monitor and to distribute health care services (Luker and Orr, 1992). All aspects of NHS spending were under scrutiny and efficiency savings were being sought at every opportunity (Holliday, 1992).

None of this is surprising when we reflect on the often expressed scepticism of Margaret Thatcher about state-run services. According to one commentator she 'never identified with the ideals of the NHS as a public service. Health was a business and as such could learn from the private sector about value for money, service and satisfying "customer" choice.' (Dickson, 1990). It is no surprise then that the reform of NHS management followed.

The introduction of general management was a necessary first part of NHS change, a prerequisite for the further changes to be brought in later, subsequent to the NHS review of 1988. If the Government wanted to run a market in health care, they needed business people at the helm to make it happen. An inquiry team was set up, therefore, to look at NHS management and to advise the Health Secretary on what action was needed.

General management and the 1983 Management Inquiry

The report of the NHS Management Inquiry Team under the chairmanship of Roy Griffiths (Managing Director of Sainsbury's) (Griffiths, 1993) was published on 25 October 1983. Norman Fowler (Secretary of State for Health) announced in the House of Commons that he accepted the general tenor of their findings and recommendations. The Inquiry Team, consisting largely of business people, had found at all levels 'a lack of clearly defined general management function with responsibility too rarely placed on one person' (Fowler, 1983). As Griffiths expressed it in his inquiry report – 'if Florence Nightingale were carrying her lamp through the corridors of the NHS today, she would almost certainly be searching for the people in charge.'

The team proposed a series of changes aimed at making the existing organization work better, which included the identification of general managers regardless of discipline at Regional, District and Unit levels of the organization. The general manager would be the final decision-maker for issues normally delegated to the consensus management team. This approach, which had existed since the inception of the NHS, was believed by the Inquiry Team to lead to 'lowest common denominator decisions, and long delays in the management process'. As Griffiths put it in yet another of his colourful analogies – 'To the outsider the NHS is so structured as to resemble a mobile: designed to move with any breath of air, but which in fact never changes its position and gives no clear indication of direction.'

Whilst denials were made that these proposals represented yet another restructuring of the service, the long-term intentions of the Government were as yet unclear. As far as the Health Secretary, Norman Fowler, was concerned at this stage he displayed clear enthusiasm for the recommendations because 'the NHS is one of the largest undertakings in western Europe. The Service needs and deserves the very best management we can give it. One of the best contributions we can make to patient care is the improvement in National Health Service Management along the lines recommended by the Griffiths' Report.'

Reaction to the Griffiths' report

The bodies representing major staff groups in the NHS appeared to accept the team's critique of management but criticized the introduction of the general manager concept. Representative bodies for nurses (the Royal College of Nursing (RCN), the Royal College of Midwives (RCM), the Association of Nursing Administrators (ANA) and the Health Visitors' Association (HVA)) saw the report as a snub to the nursing profession (Social Services Committee, 1983–84). Nurses were only mentioned twice in the Inquiry Report, that is: (1) a facetious remark about Florence Nightingale, and (2) in a passing reference to manpower levels. No real recognition was given to their important role within the NHS, and nowhere in the report was there any recommendation that a senior nurse should have one of the top managerial jobs. The annoyance of the nurse representatives was further compounded by the realization that

Griffiths had flattered and encouraged support from the medical profession by referring to them as the 'natural managers at Unit Level'. So, not only had the nursing profession been badly ignored by Griffiths, but the nurse managers already in post were not even seen as contenders for general manager posts. Nurses were outraged at the idea of being managed by a non-health professional who, they felt, would be unable to make decisions on effective patient care, as they believed 'nurses can only be led and managed by nurses'.

The Association of Nursing Administrators considered the general manager concept as 'impractical, potentially disruptive and divisive in application' (Social Services Committee 1983/84). Whilst enthusing about 'rigorous management' and 'crisper decision-making' they defended the well-established consensus management style of the NHS. They implicitly criticized the inquiry team and their commercial approach to management. Unlike a commercial organization with profit-making as a clear objective, they believed the NHS 'can never have a goal any more closely defined than, for example, 'the best use of health resources' or 'better health for the whole population'. They concluded by saying 'Decision-making in the NHS needs to be a consensus activity, in which the professional and other specialist interests concerned reach agreement on priorities and policy, and failure in a few areas is not reason to jettison the entire system'. But, in spite of all the anti-General Management comments by a wide range of health professionals including nurses, the new system was introduced.

By the end of the 1980s many NHS employees had had their battles with NHS management and the Secretary of State. Nursing staff had gained some representation in the management hierarchy, but in general had to concede the principle of professional self-government. There was much employee discontent, with nurses amongst many others taking well-reported industrial action in 1988.

A recurrent theme around all the debates was that of underfunding of the service. The Presidents of the Medical Royal Colleges gave a warning that acute hospital services were reaching crisis point because of cumulative underfunding (Hoffenberg *et al.*, 1987). Wards were having to close, and seriously ill babies were amongst those who were not receiving treatment because of staff and other resource shortages (Butler, 1992).

The Government needed to draw together all these issues, to provide a political solution which would show leadership and vision, and to prove that the NHS was still safe in their hands. Margaret Thatcher did this, just as we have seen earlier, by announcing the review of the NHS during a BBC TV programme. According to Turner 'within weeks it was evident that this gamble was paying off . . . claims of cumulative underfunding and a complete ministerial muddle were eclipsed by a coherent plan' (Turner, 1988).

The review period – opinions on offer

Clearly much debate ensued about the Government's intentions, and also a variety of opinions were offered as to the correct diagnosis and prescription. Clay, for example, looked to extra funding and an overhaul of existing NHS structures, as a good way forward. He expressed opposition to those who looked to more radical change, perhaps to systems like those in the USA. He argued that 'To have value, alternative structures must provide a better service or, at least, provide the same service at a lower cost . . .' 'Private health insurance', he claimed, 'is expensive to administer, discriminates against the elderly, the poor and the chronically sick and, in the USA has left 40 million people with no medical cover at all' (Clay, 1988).

Others disagreed with such arguments and said that increased public money was not a solution. In spite of managerial reforms, progress has not been easily made and thus a new structure was needed. According to Goldsmith (1988) 'the front runner in the debate (was) the internal market where cash follows the patient'. He offered a variety of managed health care ideas which he suggested would provide better working conditions, and a requirement to produce better quality, client-orientated health care, which is still free at the point of need. He believed that 'every pound put in would then genuinely result in a pound's worth of benefit to the patient rather than fifty penceworth that (appeared) to be provided' at that time.

The Government's strategy

Only one year after the announcement of the review, the presentation of the Government's strategy for the Health Service was made to the House of Commons (Department of Health, 1989a). The contents of the White Paper, *Working for Patients*, coupled with those of the Griffiths' Management Inquiry (1983), provided the template for the greatest change in the NHS since its inception in 1948. Whilst the NHS was acknowledged to have provided the seedbed for tremendous advances in medical technology, and a growing menu for treatments to meet the ever-rising demands for health care, this had led to problems. The cost of keeping up with it all was seen as a bit like pouring money down the perpetual black hole. A new way forward had to be adopted.

The general management changes introduced to the Health Service in 1984 were seen as a great improvement and very relevant to the late twentieth century. However, new management information systems had revealed clear variations in provision and performance across the country, wide differences in costs, drug prescribing habits, waiting times for operations, and in referrals for hospital care by GPs. Whilst there were areas of excellence, the Government stated its intent to raise all hospital and general practice standards to that of the best. They wanted to:

- Give patients, wherever they live in the UK, better health care and greater choice of services available; and
- Give greater satisfaction and rewards to those working in the NHS who successfully respond to local needs and preferences.

Nurses could of course hardly disagree with these objectives, or indeed with many of the other pious statements which characterize the Government document. It might be worth sifting back through similar health documents of the 1950s, 60s and 70s to remind ourselves that all Secretaries of State for Health have stated similar-sounding worthy objectives. What we need to do is to blow away the froth on top of this particular White Paper and examine the substance. We need to note the problems highlighted, and the solutions on offer, because the means of achieving the changes, and how they are impacting upon nurse practice and client care are central to our concerns today.

Problems needing solutions

There were a number of issues raised of great concern to the public which the Government perceived as requiring immediate attention:

1 People still sometimes have to wait too long for treatment and may have little, if any, choice over the time or place at which treatment is given.
2 The service provided on admission to hospital is sometimes too impersonal and inflexible.

It was suggested that all hospitals should provide:

- appointments' systems which are reliable;
- quiet and pleasant waiting and other public areas, with proper facilities for parents with children and for counselling worried parents and relatives;
- clear information leaflets about the facilities available and what patients need to know when they come into hospital;
- clearer, easier and more sensitive procedures for making suggestions for improvements and, if necessary, complaints;
- once someone is in hospital, clear and sensitive explanations of what is happening – on practical matters, such as where to go and who to see, and on clinical matters, such as the nature of an illness and its proposed treatment;
- rapid notification of the results of diagnostic tests; and
- a wider range of optional extras and amenities for patients who want to pay for them – such as single rooms, personal telephones, televisions and a wider choice of meals.

Whilst the last point could be seen by some as describing a two-tier service, the other ideas are clearly less contentious. They look to provide a user-friendly, quality service. Experience suggests that the NHS organization and health professionals alike have failed to run and deliver that sort of health service. All the issues raised need attention whether applied to the hospital setting or to the community.

Many would feel that in themselves all the problems listed so far could have been solved without any drastic reform of the NHS. However, the White Paper was offering major solutions to the problems of funding and controlling a state institution which the Government perceived as being grossly out of hand. The Government therefore introduced seven key ways of achieving their objectives. These included in brief:

1 The delegation of power and responsibility to local levels
  – to include greater flexibility in pay and conditions of staff.
2 The creation of self-governing status for hospitals
  – to be called Trusts.
3 The removal of administrative barriers to enable patients to travel to hospitals of their choice and which best meet their needs – money to follow patients throughout the Health Service.
4 The reduction of waiting list times, both for out-patient and in-patient care by the appointment of more consultants.
5 The ability of large general practices to become budget-holders and to compete for patients by offering better services than other practices.
6 The continued improvement of NHS business management effectiveness by the streamlining of management bodies at Regional, District and Family Practitioner levels.
7 The application of rigorous auditing to ensure quality of service and value for money activity throughout the service.

The details of all the major changes were to be published in a series of working papers (Department of Health, 1989b), shortly after the White Paper was presented to the House of Commons. Otherwise, the document gave a reasonable flavour of what was to happen in the future. Whilst freeing up the structures and activity of the NHS organization, the Government also gave explicit support to private sector care, and looked to a new partnership between the public and private sectors.

The Government believed that the NHS and independent sector had much to learn from each other, providing both mutual support and services. Any work taken from the NHS, they argued, would not only relieve pressure on it, but offer greater diversity in provision and choice for all. Indeed, the expectation was that there would be further increases in the number of people using private health care services. Again, these points smack of explicit support for a two-tier service, and perhaps even look to potential health care privatization in some form or other for the future.

All in all, whatever the intentions at this stage, the success of all the proposed changes hinged upon the new model for health care provision and purchasing – the internal health care market.

The internal health care market

Within this model of health care distribution, the purchasers of health care (District Health Authorities, GP budget holding practices and private patients) are split from the providers of health care (Health Authority Directly Managed Units, self-governing Trusts, private sector). This relationship is referred to as the purchaser–provider split . . . like in shopping! The idea is based on the belief that the competitive environment engendered between the purchasers and the providers will stimulate greater efficiency, raise standards of care and service, and thus place the patient centre stage as the powerful consumer, making choices as to which provider should receive his/her custom or patronage. The origins of such a concept are drawn from the work of the American health economist, Alan Enthoven (Robinson, 1989). Some might feel a little uneasy at equating a person seeking health care with someone shopping for other goods. Buying biscuits and clothes is, by definition, different from visiting the doctor or going to hospital. However, we will return to this when we discuss health care consumers in a later chapter. In the meantime, we will look briefly at two of the proposed changes – firstly, the hospital trusts, and secondly, the budget-holding general practices.

The hospital trusts – the new providers

One of the important aspects of the creation of the internal health care market was the proposal that as many major acute hospitals (more than 250 beds) as wish to, should run their own affairs whilst remaining part of the NHS. They would be called hospital trusts. Whilst many people will have heard them frequently referred to as opted-out hospitals (i.e. not part of the NHS arrangements), this has been repeatedly refuted. As Clarke said in the NHS Review Statement to the House of Commons in January 1989:

> Let me make it absolutely clear that they will still be as much within the NHS as they are now. They will be no freer to leave the NHS as they are now. They will be no freer to leave the NHS as any unit has been throughout its forty-year history (Clarke, 1989a).

The perceived advantages of trust status included:

- a stronger sense of local ownership and pride;
- an opportunity to build on the enormous fund of good-will that exists in local communities;

- the stimulation of commitment and the harnessing of skills of those who provide the services;
- the encouragement of local initiatives; and
- the development of a greater competitive spirit.

The idea was that hospital trusts would be encouraged to take their own decisions without detailed supervision by District and Regional Health Authorities and the Department of Health. They would be expected to negotiate staff pay rates. They would be able to make contracts to provide care for any purchasers within the NHS, or from the private sector. Subject to the constraints of providing some local essential services, as defined by statute, they would otherwise be able to compete for 'trade' in the national health care market. As finance would now follow patients across authority or regional boundary, the trusts, along with all their new freedoms to manage their own businesses, were bound to redefine and restructure the provision of NHS hospital care. According to the White Paper the Hospital Trusts would ensure 'a better deal for the public, improving the choice and quality of the services offered and the efficiency with which those services are delivered.'

The budget-holding general practice – the new-purchasers

A second proposed major change involved some general practices, if large enough, (with lists of initially at least 11 000) becoming budget holders; and thus taking responsibility for purchasing health care services for their patients from either NHS or private sector hospitals. The GPs were seen as having a crucial role in two respects: firstly, in advising patients and secondly, in ensuring that it was the patients who benefited from the reformed Health Service.

By building on the changes in general practice as set out in the earlier White Paper on primary health care

(Department of Health, 1987), the new freedoms of activity, it was argued, would allow budget-holding practices to secure better value for money, improve standards of care, offer greater consumer choice, and ensure shorter waiting times for hospital referral and admission for their patients. Practice budgets would encourage shopping around for the best services and employing the right sort of staff to meet the specific needs of the practice. In addition to this, the ability to advertise and develop available practice expertise and services would help attract more patients and thus more money. Savings made because of efficient budgeting could be ploughed back into the practice both to raise standards of service and also to enrich the potential of general practice work for those involved.

All of the activities described, it was said, would create and sharpen the competitive edge to general practice, and would raise standards as practices would have a clear financial incentive to compete against each other for patients. In addition to this, there was a clear knock-on effect in terms of hospital care from whatever sector. GPs with budgets would only refer to those hospitals which best met the needs of their patients, and which offered them the best value for money. This in turn would create competition between hospitals to gain the contracts. The expected outcome would be raising of the standards of hospital care offered and also greater choice of hospitals for patients. The financial incentive to be part of the internal health care market action was made quite clear: 'The practices and hospitals which attract the most customers will receiver the most money.' The initial budget-holding practices were to be set up in April 1991 and would be followed by others in succeeding years as the internal health care market developed its activities.

Immediate opposition by nurses

Vociferous opposition to the proposed changes came not just from politicians on the Labour and Liberal Democrat benches (see Hansard, 31st January 1989) but from the many and varied nurse interest groups. As one newspaper put it:

> A wall of professional opposition already stands between the Government and the Health Service. It begins to look more impregnable day by day. Hospital consultants, nurses and GPs are all opposed to the Government's proposed restructuring of the NHS. So are their institutions: not just their unions – the BMA, NUPE and COHSE – but nine Royal Medical Colleges and the Royal College of Nursing as well (Editorial, Guardian, 1989).

According to Clay (1989a), proposed reforms were not seen as tackling the new health agenda but preoccupied with issues of management and financial accountability.

It was acknowledged by many that the market philosophy would increasingly change the character of the NHS in ways which were unpredictable at that stage. Rowden (1989) and many other nurse commentators also, drew attention to the possibility of cost-cutting exercises, the avoidance of caring for vulnerable or chronically ill people to avoid high long-term expenditure, the increasing workload of nurses outside hospital coping with enlarging popular practices, quicker and sicker discharges from hospital following a speedier through-put of clients after surgery, and even the possibility of nurses being employed as 'mini-doctors' to reduce medical costs. The fears and concerns were many at this stage, and without a doubt prophetic.

The Working Papers (Department of Health, 1989)

Further details of the major changes which were set out in the eight Working Papers published after the White Paper were greeted with yet more opposition.

In a strongly worded statement following their publication, Trevor Clay, Royal College of Nursing General Secretary, said:

> These papers leave too many questions unanswered. It appears that the brakes are off. A much wider range of hospitals and even community services will be able to opt for trust status (Clay, 1989b).

The debate was clearly developing fast and furiously both for and against the proposals. No one working in the NHS will have failed to notice it!

Calls for nurses to stop the progress of the reforms were made because, as argued by Storey, RCN President, in April 1989: 'The package as a whole jarred against fundamental NHS principles of equity, comprehensiveness and balance' (Storey, 1989). However, the Health Secretary at the very same Conference said: 'No one should have any doubt that the reforms of the National Health Service are going to happen' (Clarke, 1989b).

By this stage, many who opposed the reforms, both public and health professionals alike, were engaging themselves in campaigns using all possible media outlets in their workplaces, and via local and national protest groups. Nurse and doctor representative organizations played their part highlighting concerns about reductions in standards of care, a need for more resources and fears for the future of the NHS. Opposition politicians took the arguments to the floor of the House of Commons and challenged the Health Secretary at every available opportunity.

Government supporters in turn described opposition tactics as 'misinformation and lying attacks, a mindless barrage of propaganda and an outrageous campaign of frightening little old ladies' (Rawnsley, 1989). The Health Secretary, in response, reiterated time after time promises of success for the reforms. He argued that:

Doctors will not run out of money, preventing them from prescribing treatments; GPs will not be under pressure to devote less time to patients; essential local hospital services will be safeguarded, quality of care, not cost will be the decisive factor in doctors' decision-making; and the Government's commitment to the health service is absolute and will remain so (Clarke, 1989c).

By July 1989 Kenneth Clarke had written to all levels of management to request that they ensure their staff were kept fully informed of the true nature of the changes so as to avoid staff being upset by persistent rumours and misinformation promulgated by anti-Government commentators.

One doctor had resigned from his long-term membership of the BMA arguing that 'frightening the patient is not part of the Hippocratic oath'. He felt the BMA campaign had created specious fears about whether or not people, particularly the elderly, would have to travel hundreds of miles to get a hospital bed, or whether their doctors would be able to offer to prescribe drugs they needed (Lockley, 1989).

The discussions and arguments were further fired by the publication of *Caring for People* (Department of Health, 1989c). Community care plans were also going to follow the market approach to purchasing and providing care. Not surprisingly, accusations again flowed as to the applicability of this model to the provision of community care. In addition to this, the effective split being created between health and social care provision was seen as fraught with untold problems.

One example to consider is that of health authority

employed Community Mental Handicap nurses. They in particular at this stage began to feel seriously under threat as nurse professionals, and also concerned for the future care of their client group. This move to split care into health and social remits clearly reflected a belief by the Government that social care could and should be provided by non-professionally qualified carers. This ignored the clear links between health and social care in helping dependent, but not ill people, maintain an independent life-style in the community setting. It also surely represented the chipping away and downgrading of qualified specialist nurse expertise. A more general discussion around this will continue in a later chapter. Meanwhile, we will return to the arguments around the new NHS reforms.

1990: A new year and new arguments

Headlines of concern followed one after another as the debate hotted up around the introduction of the NHS internal health care market with its purchasers and providers. The budget-holding notion for GPs was seen as flawed according to a group of American health experts. They argued that 'The Government's proposals require changes if they are to work as expected and are not to jeopardise standards of patient care' (Brindle, 1990a).

In March, further fuel was added to the flames when it was announced that 'outsiders had been brought in to drive through the Government's controversial health reforms' (Brindle, 1990b). However, one appointee to the Chair of South Manchester District Health Authority with clear management experience in brewing said, 'The NHS is not a business, but that does not mean it cannot benefit from business methods. More services and improved quality would result from increasing efficiency and encouraging customer awareness.'

The NHS and Community Care Act 1990

In June 1990 the NHS and Community Care Act became law. The acrimonious debates continued, particularly when it was announced in July that the Community Care changes would be phased in over three years to start formally in April 1993. On the other hand, the internal health care market was to start the following year in April 1991, without pilot or trials. Some thought that it was a very unscientific way of doing things and certainly contrary to normal good practice in the NHS.

The preparations for the new internal market arrangements developed quickly during the following months. Interestingly, the new Health Secretary, William Waldegrave, expressed some concern at the business jargon which appeared to be over-running the NHS. One commentator queried the ability of patients of the future being able 'to tell the difference between a hospital and a supermarket. Whilst there were no waiting lists at ASDA or Sainsbury, the language used by those in charge of the NHS was becoming very similar to that used in shops' (Editorial, *Nursing Times*, 1990). Indeed, another commented that 'the White Paper itself contains more choice examples of language which reduces the whole process of health care to movements of money and the generation of paperwork' (Downe, 1990).

By March 1991 the NHS was poised for lift-off. But, behind the outward show from Government of a smooth and purposeful transition, lay apparently a great deal of chaos, confusion and uncertainty. The earlier suggested promise of a truly sharp competitive edge to the new health care purchaser–provider relationships had slowly been calmed down, both in the language used by Government, and also in what was to be allowed to happen in the first year. According to Butler (1992) there was to be 'smooth continuity with the past rather than sharp divergence from it.' It was clearly felt imperative that there should be as few obvious embarrassments or problems for the Government during year one of the introduction of the changes. The market approach could not be allowed to let rip – yet. By March 1991 the NHS was ready for a 'steady' lift off. It had the structures, the management with business skills – but did it have the support of the staff?

Feelings before lift-off – 1 April 1991

According to a survey of nursing staff many were voicing concern on the eve of the reforms (Snell and Gaze, 1991):

- 60% of nurses questioned believed reforms would not improve patient care;
- over half questioned were against the reforms;
- a large proportion felt that nursing would suffer at the ward/unit and district level after 1 April 1991;
- nurses in Wales feared the impact of purchaser–provider split contracts had been underestimated;
- staff in Cardiff claimed a night dialysis service was under threat because it was expensive and uncompetitive in the new purchaser–provider world;
- staff in North-West Surrey Health Authority working in the mental handicap unit were confused and concerned about the prospect of trust status;
- in Trent, COHSE members confirmed their opposition to reforms; and
- nurses in Scotland expressed the hope that they would be able to learn from mistakes in England and Wales as they did not implement their changes until April 1992.

Clearly, whilst these points only represent some of the comments made, they do give a feel of the concern expressed by many nurses.

On 31 March the Health Secretary tried to reassure:

> There is going to be a great deal of talk. The turmoil is going to make a lot of people uncomfortable. But I'm confident that it will come out right in the end (Waldegrave, 1991).

Whilst it is not clear when 'the end' is to be, it is possible to reflect on our experiences so far and to consider future implications. A quick look at some of the press headlines may put in context the apparent success, or otherwise, of the internal health care market both for the NHS and its patients.

1 April and onwards in 1991

By May it was reported that the Government's new health market in the NHS was running into serious difficulties, and patients were paying the price. Huge variations in the cost of operations became apparent, and an embryonic two-tier system emerged in general practice with the budget-holders getting better deals for their patients at the expense of non-fund-holders. Patient choice was being restricted also, because their health authorities did not have contracts with the specific hospitals of their choice (Ferriman, May 1991).

One District Health Authority in Kent would not pay for a woman to have a sterilization operation in Guy's Hospital and another woman in Lothian was refused in vitro fertilization (Harman, 1991a). Family doctors in Coventry were told that even if patients had spent years on waiting lists, they should not be referred outside contracted hospitals. The contracting issue was also raising ethical questions. The Chairman of the senior consultants' body said that hospital consultants who agree to give preference to patients whose GPs are budget holders could be referred to the

General Medical Council for unethical conduct (Mihill, 1991). The Health Secretary acknowledged that the changes were indeed bringing about inequalities but that all the unfairness thrown up should be borne because of the eventual benefits (Travis, 1991).

Support for the Government

A leading Conservative health advisor (Baroness Cumberlege) spoke out against all the opposition to change, accusing those who did this of destroying the NHS:

> My concern is that the NHS is in danger of following the path of British Leyland: every union is scoring points by denigrating the service; market share is declining; confidence is ebbing, we are following that awful downhill path to self-destruction that has been trodden before (Brindle, 1991a).

Some might perceive that this was a novel way of deflecting blame away from some of the negative reports of the Government's reforms – the unhappy outcomes of which stayed firmly on the agenda. Whilst NHS changes were accused of 'hampering health care', (Brindle, 1991b), the Government's own research published shortly after came up with very different conclusions.

1992 – good news, bad news

At the beginning of the year the DOH circulated reports showing that patients believed trusts were a good thing, and also that the reforms in the first six months were found to be working successfully (NHS Management Executive, 1991; Hamblin, 1992). However, for many the headline 'Fury of Tory Surgeon Who Says Reforms Killed Patients' (Ferriman, 1992) seemed in sharp contrast to the Government's own report and assessment.

The gradual build-up to the April General Election started well before the announcement of it by the Prime Minister. The NHS changes had provided the meat of political debate for all the major parties for months.

The General Election – April 1992

The campaign itself highlighted arguments both for and against the NHS reforms. Many will remember the furore over the 'Jennifer's ear' story (Hencke, 1992). Whilst it has been suggested that it could have rebounded on the Labour Party, nonetheless it highlighted some of the problems of the internal health care market, including the inequities of care provision already noted, and the alleged immorality of a two-tier health care system which allows those with money to jump the queue, whilst others are forced to wait. The outcome of the General Election, however, ensured that all was 'full steam ahead' in the NHS. The Conservative Government had been given another five years to develop their internal health care market.

1993 and beyond?

The earlier proposals for developing relationships with the independent sector in providing health care went one step further. Guy's Hospital Trust was to provide McDonald's with the 460th UK restaurant. Many agreed that this partnership was most strange:

> The NHS is the antithesis of most of what McDonald's stands for: it is not possible to get much further from the ideals of American capitalism. The NHS concerns are solemn ones of health and disease, life and death. McDonald's business revolved around an object which is trivial and frivolous (Davies, 1993).

Bizarre thought all this may appear, it reflects the growing commercialism of many parts of the NHS which the new internal market has supported. Sometimes it is difficult to know whether you are in a shopping mall or Out-Patients when you visit some hospitals. It is also ironic to reflect on the Government's often expressed concern about NHS bureaucracy and its cost. Figures were published in January 1993 to show that:

> More than 18 000 extra managers and office staff were appointed by the National Health Service in England when the Government introduced its market style health care system. Around 8500 nursing jobs disappeared at the same time (Brindle, 1993).

The experience of nurses both in hospital or community over the past two or three years would surely back up these figures. Nurse representatives have repeatedly challenged the Health Secretary to shift the balance back, so that nurses can give the high standard of care for which they are educated and as promised by the reforms. The debate around these issues looks set to continue, judging by the nursing press.

In conclusion, this brief discussion of the NHS reforms and the internal health care market still inevitably – given the short time since implementation – leaves many questions unanswered:

1 Has the creation of an internal health care market been good or bad for the NHS and what is likely to happen in the future?
2 Are nurses being enabled to give the higher standards of care as promised by the White Paper?
3 Have the NHS reforms dealt with the problem of underfunding?

4 Has the new system redefined the role and responsibilities of nurses?

5 Have the users of the NHS benefited as promised?

These questions are all part of political debate. They are all equally relevant to nurses, as professionals, in determining whether the reformed NHS provides a context in which the shared and communal values of nursing can now be effectively implemented.

The discussion in the following chapters will hopefully go some way towards clarifying what has been happening, and to plan our response to the changes and challenges facing all nurses wherever they work within the NHS.

References

Benner Patricia (1991) The Storyteller. *Nursing Times*, **87**(38).

Black Sir Douglas (1980) *Inequalities in Health: Report of a Research Working Group*. London, HMSO.

Brindle David (1990a) Budget Plan for G.P.'s 'flawed'. *The Guardian*, January 26.

Brindle David (1990b) Outsiders picked to oversee health service changes. *The Guardian*, March 12.

Brindle David (1991a) Health chief wars of NHS path to ruin. *The Guardian*, June 7.

Brindle David (1991b) NHS changes 'hampering health care'. *The Guardian*, November 7.

Brindle David (1993) Market is strangling NHS with red tape, MP claims. *The Guardian*, January 7.

Butler John (1992) *Patients, Policies and Politics*. Milton Keynes, Open University Press.

Central Statistical Office (1993) *Social Trends 23*. London, HMSO.

Clarke Kenneth MP (1989a) *Statement NHS Review*. Hansard, January 31 **146**(39).

Clarke Kenneth in Brindle David (1989b) Reforms will go forward, Clarke warns nurses. *The Guardian*, April 4.

Clarke Kenneth in Brindle David (1989c) Clarke tells GPs of leaflet errors. *The Guardian*, April 20.

Clay Trevor (1988) What Treatment Does the NHS Need? *Nursing Times*, **84**(16).

Clay Trevor (1989a) Clay on the Review. *Nursing Times*, **85**(6).

Clay Trevor (1989b) in News: Working Papers 'a backward step' say nursing unions. *Nursing Times*, **85**(9).

Cook Robin M.P. (1989) *Statement NHS Review* Hansard, January 31 **146**(39).

Davies Peter (1993) Why Guy's is out to lunch. *Health Service Journal*, January 7.

Department of Health (1987) *Promoting Better Health*. Cmnd. 249. London, HMSO.

Department of Health (1989a) *Working For Patients*. Cmnd. 555. London, HMSO.

Department of Health (1989b) *National Health Service Review Working Papers*. (Package of 8 Booklets). London, HMSO.

Department of Health (1989c) *Caring For People*. Cmnd. 849. London, HMSO.

Dickson Niall (1990) The Thatcher legacy. *Nursing Times*, **86**(48).

Downe Soo (1990) Ward power. *Nursing Times*, **86**(16).

Editorial (Guardian) (1989) The support is not there. *The Guardian*, March 28.

Editorial (Nursing Times) (1990) Comment. *Nursing Times*, **86**(51).

Editorial (Nursing Times) (1992) Comment. *Nursing Times*, **88**(16).

Ferriman Annabel (1991) Patients pay price of the market. *Sunday Observer*, May 5.

Ferriman Annabel (1992) Fury of Tory surgeon who says reforms killed patients. *Sunday Observer*, February 9.

Foot Michael (1973) *Aneurin Bevan*. Vol 2. London, Davis Poynter.

Fowler Norman (1983) *Hansard – Issue 1286 (24th–28th October)*. October 25, p. 168.

Gaze Harriet (1990) Sweeping change? *Nursing Times*, June 13 **86**(24).

Goldsmith Michael (1988) The case for a radical overhaul *Nursing Times*, April 20 **84**(16).

Griffiths Roy (1983) *NHS Management Inquiry*. Letter to Norman Fowler. London, Department of Health.

Hamblin Martin (1992) *Attitudes Among Patients Leaving Trust Hospitals*. London, Department of Health.

Harman Harriet MP (1991a) Reform that will end in tiers. *The Guardian*, May 21.

Harman Harriet MP (1991b) Bad medicine for the NHS. *The Guardian*, November 7.

Hencke David (1992) Couple divided on broadcast. *The Guardian,* March 26.

Hoffenberg R, Todd IP and Pinker G (1987) Crisis in the National Health Service. *British Medical Journal*, **295**(1505).

Holliday Ian (1992) *The NHS Transformed*. Manchester, Baseline Books.

Hunter David (1993) To Market! To Market! A new dawn for community care. *Health and Social Care In The Community*. **1**(1).

Laurent Claire (1990) Taken to the cleaners? *Nursing Times*, **86**(19).

Lockley Dr. John (1989) Advice from the BMA that patients should ignore. *The Guardian*, September 18.

Luker K and Orr J (eds) (1992) *Health Visiting. Towards Community Health Nursing*. Oxford, Blackwell Scientific Publications.

Mihill Chris (1991) NHS contract deal raises ethics threat. *The Guardian*, May 4.

NHS Management Executive (1991) *NHS Reforms. The First Six Months*. London, HMSO.

Rawnsley Andrew (1989) Overweight Health Minister ignores doctors' orders. *The Guardian*, April 26.

Robinson Ray (1989) New health care market. *British Medical Journal*, **298** 437–439.

Rowden Ray (1989) What's in it for us? *Nursing Times*, **85**(8).

Snell J and Gaze H (1991) Staff across the UK voice concern on the eve of health service reform. *Nursing Times*, **87**(13).

Social Services Commitee (1984) *Griffiths NHS Management Inquiry Report*, 1983–84. HC 209, HMSO, London.

Storey Maude in Brindle David (1989) Reforms will go forward, Clarke warns nurses. *The Guardian*, April 4.

Travis Alan (1991) Health Secretary admits new inequalities. *The Guardian*, May 27.

Turner Toni (1988) The last nail. *Nursing Times*, **84**(16).

Waldegrave William in Koenig P, Kingman S and Sage A (1991) The NHS and you. *The Independent on Sunday*, March 31.

Welch Colin (1993) Now the bourgeoisie bang their spoons. *The Independent*, May 31.

Whitehead Margaret (1987) *The Health Divide: Inequalities in Health in the 1980's*. London, Health Education Authority.

3

The NHS and the Consumers

One alleged purpose of the recent reforms of the National Health Service has been to provide patients with better quality care and a wider choice of services. The then Prime Minister's foreword was clear in that all the proposals in the White Paper (Department of Health, 1989) were designed to put the needs of the patient first. This was a continuation of the Government's previously stated desire to strengthen the consumer's position through increased information for users and competition amongst providers (Department of Health, 1987).

The new style consumer responsiveness implied by the changes, both for nurses, and other NHS employees, is of interest. But is it new? At one level, putting the patient first has always been central to nurse caring, and the latest code of professional conduct (UKCC, 1992), reaffirms that 'the primacy of the interests of patients or clients, remains quite properly the dominant theme' (Pyne, 1992). So, what does the new NHS model offer the consumers which is better than before? The following discussion may help to find some answers.

This chapter, then, will examine the thesis about enhanced consumer choice and power. In order to come to a conclusion as to whether recent changes in the NHS have added to consumer power, we will turn to the political dis-enchantment and consumer dissatisfaction which emerged around the debates on the NHS in the 1980s. Finally, we

will discuss the changes which have been introduced with
the use of market language, and the emphasis upon the individual consumer.

As we move through the evidence and the arguments, we
will then conclude that, essentially, a market-led health care
system could potentially add to inequalities in provision,
and that, in any case, a system which is based upon a vicar-
ious relationship between the individual and the provider
cannot be guaranteed to add to consumer choice. Finally,
and against this background, we will look at the consumer
argument, and the changes which have taken place, and
how these relate to the role, and the professionalizing of
nurses.

Stirrings of Political Disenchantment

Governments of all political persuasions accepted and
indeed promoted the development of the NHS until the
early 1980s. The 1979 election promises of reduced public
expenditure, decreased taxation and thus more choice and
freedom for individuals to spend their incomes as they
wished, were clear signs to a new direction in health and
spending policy. It was obvious that many of the electorate
liked the messages which they heard, and gave strong support for a different approach to health care which, as we
now know, was to have profound implications for the NHS,
nurses, and by definition, for all the consumers of the health
services. Few nurses will be unaware of the changes since
then, with the creation of new structures, a different style of
management coupled with the language of the market
place, and the stated purpose to please the consumer.

The most recent changes as we know from the last chapter have occurred following the implementation of the
NHS and Community Care Act 1990. Some have likened

the reforms to the beginnings of a privatized health care system (Cook, 1989), something like in the United States (Cairns-Berteau, 1991). Some were delighted that such a radical overhaul was taking place (Goldsmith, 1988) and others are presently working at developing ever more complex changes to work towards an even more market orientated health service (Brindle, 1993). However the reforms were described, and whatever their future potential, the consumer was alleged to be the central focus for all activity within the NHS internal health care market.

So, what had the old style NHS failed to deliver for consumers, and what challenges did the new NHS need to meet to achieve success?

Market language and the implications for consumers

The new reforms were intended to have a clear market feel about them, and to emphasize the opportunity for patients to demand and to expect the services which they desire. Conversely, those health care providers who failed to meet these successfully, would lose out financially as patients went elsewhere to meet their choices for care. The Government clearly stated that it would make it possible for the money to be available to treat patients, to move freely to the hospitals which offer patients the best service and the best value for money (Department of Health, 1989).

Whilst, however, much of the language of the reforms clearly suggest a sort of market relationship between the purchasers and providers of health care in the NHS it is strange that the word consumer is never used in the White Paper to describe the users of the service. Some commentators have remarked on its surprising absence because:

> By using the terms 'patient' and 'consumer' as if they were interchangeable, the document not only suggests a narrow

conception of the NHS role; it also lacks a framework within which to identify the full range and diversity of consumer interests in the health field (Harrison *et al*, 1989).

Indeed the title of the White Paper itself *Working for Patients* similarly reflects this apparent limited remit of concern.

Are we beginning then to expose some interesting potential intentions or implications for the health care of consumers? If those who consume the health services are only to be patients, that is they are unwell and in need of some medical or nursing intervention, what about the rest of the population who are apparently fit and do not? This is an interesting point, particularly in light of the document *The Health of the Nation* (Department of Health, 1992). In it, the Secretary of State for Health, Virginia Bottomley states:

> The need to focus on health as much as health care is seen as a realisable ambition now that that reforms have made this strategic approach possible.

She continues:

> Although there is much the Government and the NHS need to do, the objectives and the targets cannot be delivered by Government and the NHS alone. They are truly – for all of us – to achieve. We must be clear about where responsibilities lie. We must get the balance right between what the Government, and the Government alone, can do, what other organisations and agencies need to do, and finally, what individuals and families themselves must contribute if the strategy is to succeed.

So is the NHS to be a service in the future which aims to concern itself only with ill consumers, and perhaps leave health promotion and education to other providers? This is an important question for nurses because of efforts made in recent years to develop new health and community focused roles. Any narrowing of their potential care arenas, to a medicalized ill-health remit, will not only inhibit nurse developments so far, but could prove to be bad news for consumers, whose health care needs in reality extend far wider than individual pathological problems and medical intervention. Perhaps then, if this is the case it could be suggested that the language of consumerism, so prevalent in the NHS today, is merely a front for what is really going on within the changes brought about by the internal health care market.

Meanwhile, as we can see in the following paragraph, some nurses, in good faith, have made efforts to use a consumer/marketized approach in their work, largely because they feel that it is here to stay – at least until a change of government calls a halt.

Kelly and Swift (1992) for example, believe that the internal health care market purchasers can learn a great deal from the private sector. They used as their example how one of the biggest high street retailers, Marks and Spencer, buy their supplies and ensure a quality product for their customers. Marks and Spencer's principles for trading, established in 1884 and restated in 1984 included:

- offering customers a selected range of goods of high quality and good value;
- working in close co-operation with suppliers;
- always buying British goods, providing the goods the British supplier produces represent high quality and good value; and
- developing and maintaining good human relationships with staff, suppliers and customers.

All of the above could be said to form the basis of a successful purchaser – provider relationship, and clearly it is of apparent benefit to the consumers of Marks and Spencer's products. So, it is not really surprising then, that such a commonsense presentation of arrangements, with the promise of good outcomes for the consumers, like in any well marketed goods – is appealing to many.

Maybe nurses need to delve further into the issue, however, before coming to a conclusion. Making any product (in this case health care) fit the needs of the consumer is important, but is this true consumerism with the customer or patient getting what they want, and really having a say in how their health care is shaped and delivered? Nurses would do well to reflect on this question because of the promise of the primacy of their client needs as expressed in the nurse professional code of conduct. We need to consider whether or not a form of true consumerism has developed, and the consumer gaining the promised benefits from the reforms.

Consumer choice – a myth or reality?

According to some the language of consumerism certainly seems to have taken root in the health service (Avis, 1992). Also, according to much of the health care literature the role of those grateful recipients of care (Klein, 1983) has been transformed in the past decade theoretically, if not in reality, to that of active consumer (Klein, 1990). In the early 1980s for example, the NHS was described by many as being more responsive to its employee needs and preferences than to those of its users. During the Management Inquiry for example (Griffiths, 1983), Sir Roy Griffiths argued that the NHS was definitely not consumer friendly. He found a lack of information about services available to users, little choice of care on offer, no easily identified channels for complaints, and little effort to find out about and involve the recipients of the service. His solution to this lack of consumer care was, as we know, a more businesslike approach in the NHS and the introduction of general management.

Griffiths believed that businessmen had a keen sense of how well they were looking after their customers, but doubted that the NHS management met the needs of the patient or the community. The medicine needed by the ailing health service was general management, so that the consumer became central to all activities, and as taxpayers, gained the best value for their money.

Developments in general management from 1984 and other health service changes implemented since then have promoted continually the centrality of the consumer's voice. In spite of this, concerns are expressed as to the genuineness of the professed commitment to the consumer and whether the reforms merely reflect a clever use of words obscuring other policy objectives which are incompatible with true consumer choice. Perhaps a judgement, on the success or not of the promised focus, might be reached by comparing those concerns expressed by users of the NHS before the changes, with some of the post-reform comment on NHS consumer activity.

Users' concerns – a case to answer?

In September 1989 a consortium of user groups set out a list of worries about the NHS which they wished to see addressed (Voluntary Organisations, 1989). The problems highlighted by them included:

- fragmentation of health services between hospitals, community services and general practitioners;

- poor co-ordination between health and local authority services so that it is easy for people to slip through the gaps;
- inequality of access to health services, both in different geographical areas and for particular disadvantaged groups, such as people from ethnic minorities and homeless people;
- lack of protection and safeguards for patients, such as in making complaints and seeking redress;
- lack of public and community involvement in decision making and planning; and
- underfunding of health services, particularly community care.

Any reform of the NHS they argued, needed to address these problems, but they doubted that this would happen. They felt that many users of the health service who were disadvantaged (e.g. those with physical disabilities, mental health problems, learning difficulties, problem drug and alcohol users and the homeless) were likely to have greater problems after the implementation of the health service changes than before. They perceived that the introduction of competition, even of a managed variety, into the NHS, was likely to throw up winners and losers. The losers they felt would probably be the most vulnerable users of the health services. It is clear then, that these consumers had many well-thought out concerns needing attention. We now need to look at some of the debate which has followed the changes in order to assess the success or not of the reforms.

Better care for the consumers?

According to an NHS Management Executive report in January 1992 'the NHS is working better than ever and the consumers gaining greater benefits than previously' (NHS Management Executive, 1992). Changes in the way the

NHS is organized had helped to re-focus activities. They were leading to improvements in the quality of care, greater responsiveness to individuals and even better value for money from the growing NHS budget. However, other commentators tell a very different story. In the last chapter we saw that rationalization and cutting of services have been very much in evidence, hospitals have closed, and also wards. Surgical activity has been slowed up or stopped because budgets have run out before the end of the financial year. Services previously available free within the NHS are now either not available or attract charges. It could be argued that such outcomes represent stringent prioritizing, rationing, and a reduced consumer choice. This result would of course be directly opposite to the professed aim of the Government's health changes.

The promise to listen to the consumers' views is also felt to be suspect. Some people believe that far from giving people more say in how their health service is run, the recent reforms actually give them less (Plamping and Delamothe, 1991). They look to the marginalization of community health councils, to the changed composition of health authority membership with little or no local representation, to the non-democratic make-up of self-governing Trusts and Family Health Service Authority management bodies (Mason, 1990; Selincourt, 1992). As an editorial in the *Guardian* put it:

> The restructuring of the NHS has not been restricted to changing the way health care is delivered. Just as seriously it has been accompanied by tighter restrictions on the release of information to the public. Under the new scheme, community health councils (CHCs) have been shunted into the sidings, and the new health authorities given far more freedom to shut out the press and the public. The new style authorities have seized on this new chance of secrecy. Medics and consumer representatives are now in a minority; the majority of

non-executive members are drawn from industry, business, the law and accountancy. A recent survey showed one out of five was only going to meet in public once a quarter. Two out of three were refusing to allow even community health council representatives to remain in the private sessions (Editorial, *Guardian*, 1991).

Some have described the promised consumerist stance as being very limited, and all about public relations, but certainly not true consumerism. As Mahon (1992) says, 'much emphasis and publicity has indeed been given to reducing waiting lists, chasing quality care, reducing costs and ever improving information flow to patients.' However, she is concerned at the vagueness of these initiatives, and how they will translate into greater choice for the consumers.

Whilst we are considering the outcomes in this way, we can profitably return again (with our eye on the consumer angle) to the workings of the internal health care market. This also is apparently not quite as it seems.

Will the real consumers stand up?

It has been said by some commentators that the activity of the internal market in the health service so far has had very little to do with increased consumer choice. We might consider the fact that in a true market situation the customer is in a direct relationship in terms of buying and choosing a product. This is not true in the NHS. The people who purchase and choose care from the provider Trusts and Directly Managed Units, are not the supposed consumers, but the health authorities and budget holding GPs who thus potentially wield great power.

In the NHS market place, the purchasing authorities and GP fundholders call the tune, and if the providers do not sing along they may lose their voice altogether (Willis, 1992).

So, as we can see, the purported consumer is not only not at the forefront of choice-making and competition, but in reality represents the currency by which improvements in efficiency and financial control of internal health markets are to be achieved. Hospitals are to be funded more directly for the volume of the services they provide, and those hospitals which offer patients the best service and the best value for money will be better rewarded than those which do not; that is the notion of money following the patient. Maybe the consumer, as a result of changes, will benefit, but not it seems as a result of being able to influence change directly.

Another point to consider as suggested by some is that the real intent of the new internal market mechanism is to make clinicians work within management objectives, to keep costs down and to push up productivity rather than meet patients' preferences (Pollitt, 1989). As Griffiths earlier in the 1980s said, 'Clinicians must participate fully in decisions about priorities in the use of resources' (Griffiths, 1983).

This theme is further developed in the White Paper (Department of Health, 1989). 'The decisions taken by consultants are critical to the way in which the money available for the NHS is used. It is therefore important to ensure that consultants are properly accountable for the consequences of these decisions.' The reforms set out proposals for striking a proper balance between two legitimate pressures, both of which are focused on patients' interests: the professional responsibilities and rewards of the individual consultants, and the responsibility of managers to ensure that the money available for hospitals buys the best possible service for patients. Again the benefits of this are perceived as improving the service to consumers, but in no way is the consumer seen as participating in influencing directly any change in the amount of NHS funding monies made available – rather consumers are seen as the recipients of others' decisions and priorities. The internal market so created seems to be a structure not primarily designed to empower clients.

If as it appears the consumer is no more powerful now than previous to the changes, perhaps one might consider the inevitability of this occurrence. As already described, the collectivist NHS came into being to overcome the vagaries of failure of a market provision in health care. Why should a partial return to a market-like situation be any more successful in the 1990s? Indeed, if we also agree with Aneurin Bevan's stated belief that the NHS he helped to create could never meet all the needs of all the people either (Foot, 1973), then are we now all chasing and hoping for some illusory notion of absolute choice? This Government however does not appear to believe or even acknowledge such an idea.

Whilst promising greater choice and power from the internal market reforms introduced to the NHS, the Government has, with much publicity, armed the consumers with what could only be described as a paper chase of charters.

The charters – frills and trappings?

The charters are intended to set standards against which the public, the professionals and the politicians can check care and treatment provided by public bodies. Supposedly they would enable people to demand good quality care.

In the Foreword to the Citizen's Charter for example (HMSO, 1991), John Major wrote about making public services more answerable to their users and raising their overall quality. He saw this as part of a wider reform programme started in the 1980s which included schools, housing and health care. Four key words exemplified his plans to give people more say in how their services were run:

- quality;
- standards;
- choice;
- value.

If the consumers of the services were not happy with any of these aspects they could just go elsewhere.

These ideas were reiterated in the Patient's Charter (Department of Health, 1991) to put power in the hands of the public by highlighting for the first time their rights within the reformed health service. However Kargar (1993) is dismissive of the power of the Charter to ensure better health care for consumers. Winkler's description (1987) of NHS activity as a 'supermarket model of consumerism', fits in aptly with another's description of the Charter as 'the frills and trappings of patient power' (Editorial, *Nursing Times,* 1991). The shopping analogies which emerge time after time seem sadly particularly apt in the NHS today. It seems that the Charters are a bit like the free gifts offered by retailers – they are an encouragement to buy, but not to create the product on the shelf. Some would argue they could be seen as merely representing a cynical ploy by Government to give the public an image of power, but little weight in reality.

An examination of the 'man in the street's' views by a nurse journal reporter, a year after the publication of the Patient's Charter, found that:

> The concept of patient's rights was largely endorsed, but appeared to remain theoretical. There was widespread cynicism about whether these so-called rights were anything more than paper promises, intended more for public show than for real change (*Nursing Times,* 1992).

What is the judgement?

Is the new reformed model of NHS care, backed by its charters and full of promises really offering consumers something better than before? We need to keep in mind that the true health care consumer should surely be offered a wide variety of options, to be kept fully informed and involved in managing their care. The reader should reflect on the concerns of the user groups noted earlier, and also think about their own experiences, and decide whether the reforms have facilitated the improvements sought. Inevitably conclusions will be mixed.

Many nurses of course will rightly defend the efforts they have made in recent years to give better care, and to give consumers a stronger voice in negotiating that care. They will look to developments in both role and practice of nurses, and to increasing sensitivity and ability in providing individualized care. They will look to work on quality assurance as a way of demonstrating a genuine concern for patient interests and upholding standards of care (Pullan and Edmonds, 1992).

All of these examples should be applauded. However, the issue of promoting a true consumerist approach in the NHS surely involves a much wider remit than the apparent 'window-dressing', and 'frills and trappings' approach being offered via the reforms. According to Mahon (1992), any new development in client behaviour and expectation is going to take longer than a few years, and to need more than a new name to become in reality something significantly different. This, according to Mahon, would require 'a shift away from the harmless version of consumerism so far, towards alternative models that explore the nature of the doctor–nurse–patient relationship and embrace the concepts of involvement, empowerment and advocacy. Such a shift would require radical changes in the institutional and cultural context of health service provision.'

We surely have to acknowledge that such moves are not something being actively sought within the ongoing reforms, judging by previous findings. Indeed we need to pause and consider whether we should be working towards a full-blown consumerist approach anyway. This could herald its own unwanted repercussions. It might result in an even more unbalanced use of the health services by some of the stronger, more articulate members of society, at the expense of the less vociferous and weaker members. This could be seen to produce a model of health care distribution which is antipathetic to a national institution like the NHS, designed to meet social needs in some equitable fashion – a model within which we as nurses have grown and developed.

Similarly, one might question the idea that if people had a more representational say in the running of the health service (on FHSA–HA Management Boards) then their voices as consumers would be better heard. Again, this might not work out as expected if one reflects on research findings. The Black Report (1980) and Whitehead (1987), for example, demonstrated that the middle classes gained most from the old style NHS, not only by making their voices heard, but from having the knowledge and ability to make their demands in an articulate fashion. They did well before the changes, they are probably doing reasonably well now, and a return to the previous representational arrangements might merely return them to their previous status quo. The weakest and most vulnerable consumers would still have the lesser voice.

We might conclude that neither situation is helpful, if we aspire to provide some level of equitable provision for all the potential users of the service. In fact it seems almost inevitable that the inverse care law whereby those who need the most health care get the least, comes into play whichever way we turn. However, judging by earlier findings about the impact of the reforms, it seems that the imbalance is probably sharper than ever in favour of those who can better afford any potential increases in charging or who could pay for private care if necessity dictated. In light of the well-reported recession of the early 1990s and the high numbers unemployed, however, a large group of the population must be very concerned as the reforms develop, particularly if illness strikes them or their families. So for nurses, with a code of practice emphasizing the importance of the client, this particular debate must be of concern. To do nothing is to accept a new environment of health care provision which does not appear to reflect either a model of true consumerism, or indeed, to offer anything like a service which is in the interests of all the users.

Consumers: what is the agenda for nurses?

The discussion so far has come to the following broad conclusions. In many respects, the Government's emphasis and language have put the consumer onto the agenda in a more pronounced way than at any other time in the history of the NHS. On the other hand, it is felt that the consumer participation offered is limited and, at best, indirect, and, also potentially with a restricting definition of health equating health to illness.

It is in this contradiction that both a challenge and a risk emerge for nurses. As with apple pie and motherhood, everybody is going to be in favour of consumer choice. Nurses will be no exception, as professional values and modern practice both point in the same direction of greater negotiation between nurse and patient, and greater choice on the part of the patient. The challenge comes in terms of differentiating between the nurses' professional view of consumer choice, and the Government's language and reforms.

It it is accepted, as argued in the earlier part of this chapter, that the Government's programme for the NHS has not necessarily added to consumer choice, and, indeed with the introduction of market values and disciplines and with the argument about the levels of required funding for the NHS, access to health care might have become more socially unequal, then the agenda of consumer choice assumes a more radical dimension. Therefore nurses, and their organizations, which argue that there is a link between effective consumer choice and adequate resourcing will be faced with the task of participating in all those debates around the sufficiency and redistribution of resources within the NHS. Perhaps that is the only route if nurses are to speak with strength and conviction on behalf of their clients. They are by desire or by implication moving into a more sharply defined political agenda. Intriguingly, as we shall see, it might be the only option if nurses wish to protect and to enhance their professionalism in a market motivated NHS.

References

Avis Mark (1992) Patients's choice *Nursing Times*, **88**(30).

Black Sir Douglas (1980) *Inequalities In Health: Report Of A Research Working Group*. London, HMSO.

Brindle David (1993) Privatise NHS, urges Tory MP. *The Guardian*, April 13.

Cairns-Berteau Mary (1991) LA Flaw. *Nursing Times*, **87**(5).

Cook Robin (1989) Statement *NHS Review*. Hansard, **146**(39).

Department of Health (1987) *Promoting Better Health*. Cmd. 249. London, HMSO.

Department of Health (1989) *Working For Patients*. Cmd. 555. London, HMSO.

Department of Health (1991) *The Patient's Charter*. London, HMSO.

Department of Health (1992) *The Health of the Nation*. London, HMSO.

Editorial (Guardian) (1991) Stealthy is not very healthy. *The Guardian*, May 20.

Editorial (Nursing Times) (1991) Comment. *Nursing Times*, **87**(45).

Foot Michael (1973) *Aneurin Bevan* Vol 2. London, Davis Poynter.

Goldsmith M (1988) The case for a radical overhaul. *Nursing Times*, **84**(16).

Griffiths Roy (1983) *NHS Management Inquiry*. London, DHSS.

Harrison Steve, Hunter David, Johnston Ian and Wistow Gerald (1989) *Competing For Health. A Commentary On The NHS Review*. Nuffield Institute Reports, University of Leeds.

HMSO (1991) *The Citizen's Charter*. Cmd. 1599. London, HMSO.

Kargar Ishbel (1993) Charter of charters. *Nursing Times*, **89**(2).

Kelly Patrick and Swift Richard (1992) Quality feat. *Nursing Times*, **88**(33).

Klein Rudolf (1983) *The Politics Of The National Health Service*. London, Longman.

Klein Rudolf (1990) Looking after consumers in the new NHS. *British Medical Journal*, **300**, 1351–2.

Mahon Ann (1992) Feature. Manchester University patient survey. *Health Service Journal*, December 3.

Mason Peter (1990) Consumers' voice. *Nursing Times*, **86**(31).

NHS Management Executive (1992) *NHS Reforms. The First Six Months*. London, HMSO.

Nursing Times (1992) Power To The People. *Nursing Times*, **89**(14).

Plamping Diane and Delamothe Tony (1991) The Citizen's Charter and the NHS. *British Medical Journal*, **303**, 203–204.

Pollitt C (1989) Consuming passions. *Health Service Journal*, **99**(5178) 1436–37.

Pullan Barry and Edmonds Jane (1992) Everybody's business. *Nursing Times*, **88**(4).

Pyne Reginald (1992) Changing the Code. *Nursing Times*, **88**(25).

Selincourt Kate de (1992) Power to the patients. *Nursing Times*, **88**(33).

United Kingdom Central Council (1992) *Code of Professional Conduct For The Nurse, Midwife and Health Visitor*. 3rd. ed.

Voluntary Organisations (1989) *Health Services Users And The NHS Review*. A Statement From Voluntary Organisations. London, Health Service Users Initiative.

Whitehead Margaret (1987) *The Health Divide: Inequalities In Health In The 1980's*. London, Health Education Authority.

Willis Jenine (1992) The price of health. *Nursing Times*, **88**(30).

Winkler F (1987) Consumerism in health care: beyond the supermarket model. *Policy and Politics*, **15**(1) 1–8.

4

The NHS and Health Promotion

The promotion of the nation's health is not a late twentieth-century idea. Progress had already been made even before the well-reported sanitary revolution of the nineteenth century. Quarantine facilities and basic programmes to care for the sick were already in evidence. However, the upheavals of the industrial revolution and the creation of immense social problems provided the impetus for a more developed collective approach to the public's health, with the provision over time of clean water, sewerage systems, street lighting, better housing and immunization. If industry and thus the economic base of the country were to be thriving and healthy, it was imperative that those who worked to make it happen, were fit to play their part. As the Royal Sanitary Commission stated in 1871:

> The constant relation between the health and vigour of the people and the welfare and commercial prosperity of the state requires no argument . . . public health is public wealth (Acheson, 1988).

It was therefore increasingly accepted by Government as it moved towards the twentieth century, that there was a need for government to intervene to enhance individual efforts to be healthy. Without a doubt, the 40% rejection on medical grounds of applicants who wished to be recruited for active service in the Boer War, helped to initiate the later governmental interventions in health care. The 1919

Health Act charged the Minister of Health to take all such steps as may be desirable to secure the preparation, effective carrying out and co-ordination of measures conducive to the health of the people.

Prevention of illness and the promotion of health were clearly of great importance, and activity ranged widely in this. We see the creation of infectious disease hospitals, new general hospitals, and special services for pregnant women, mothers, babies and school children. The Minister was also extensively involved in the control of those wider environmental factors along with housing and food hygiene which, it was accepted, all affected the health of the population.

At this stage then, the determinants of health were seen as complex, multifaceted and as such were the remit and responsibility of the Health Minister and his department. A collective response to those issues was accepted as a necessary role of government. People needed to be helped to health, particularly in the control of those factors over which they could exercise little power. For example, unemployment of the 1930s and the resultant poverty and ill-health are factors which only the development of a healthy economic and industrial base could heal.

The Second World War raised questions about all previous government policy, and provided the catalyst for the new post-war creation of the Welfare State. The Beveridge plan (Beveridge, 1942) to fight the so-called giants of want, ignorance, disease, idleness and squalor, provided a post-war strategy to shape and control those powerful determinants of the public's health. Financial benefits, state education, public housing initiatives, employment creation and development, and a health service were collective responses to meet the needs of the population, and were aimed to help individuals to be healthy, and to create in turn a healthy nation.

In spite of much popular support for such developments, the post-war Labour Government had to fight tooth and nail to carry through their proposed legislation. The NHS Bill faced, as we already know, strong opposition from many members of the medical profession (Foot, 1973). Aneurin Bevan was forced to make political concessions to this very powerful professional group but, nonetheless, carried the Bill through to enactment, and thereby delivered a national health service to this country.

The new National Health Service of 1948 was not only to provide medical care, but to:

- provide an equitable distribution of health care services;
- provide services which were accountable to the nation;
- give a sense of collective purpose or mission; and importantly
- promote the health of the nation.

Along with the other structures of the welfare state, the health service would be part of a great collective enterprise made up of several branches across Government, all helping individuals to be healthy.

More than forty years on the NHS has many achievements of which to be proud in improving the nation's health. However, alongside broader social inequalities, the NHS has almost inevitably found it difficult to live up to the idealistic aspirations of its founders (Black, 1980). Accountability to the population, it seems, has been reduced, and new ill health problems have emerged which are either poorly or not addressed. The collectivist approach to health care is perceived by many as being seriously under attack, and the ongoing Conservative health policy initiatives are riddled with mixed messages. The long-term consensus by policy makers of whatever political persuasion in support of a national health service has broken down, not least because of the ever-rising costs of care and the perceived economic imperative to reduce public expenditure. No doubt also, strong support for a political perspective which is anti-collective in nature has gained strength, and has been strongly enunciated by all the Conservative Governments since the late 1970s. This has resulted in questioning by many as to the need for an NHS model of care provision which has been presented as outdated, inefficient and wasteful of taxpayers' money.

The first review of the NHS for 40 years (Department of Health, 1989a) coupled with that of community care (Department of Health, 1989c) led as we know to the enactment of the NHS and Community Care Act in June 1990. The reforms, involving profound changes in structure, organization and management of the NHS have, it is suggested enabled the Government 'to focus on health as much as health care'. Thus the backcloth to NHS activity is the latest health strategy for the nation (Department of Health, 1992a), which whilst acknowledging a multiplicity of causes of ill-health, pushes the responsibility of meeting these across the whole nation.

Questions of interest which must now emerge for nurses as health promoters must be:

1 How far do the NHS reforms promote or hinder the carrying out of this new health strategy for the nation?
2 Do the changes provide the context within which all nurses, of whatever discipline or interest, can both play their full part in promoting health, and also at the same time provide the better health care as promised by the 1990 Act?

In conclusion what might emerge is the sad reality that the health strategy though presented in glossy and attractive packaging, lacks real detail for action, clear financial backing and thus serious intent. Rather than a backcloth to the NHS changes, it is a figleaf behind which a full-frontal dismantling of the NHS is slowly taking place to become a skeletal medical and illness service. And finally, for nurses working in the NHS, role diminution will be the outcome, as the emphasis will be on providing a patching-up service, rather than being the major health promoter of the nation.

This chapter will develop a discussion around these aspects, by examining briefly some definitions of the concept of health, thereby defining our focus for care as nurses. Consideration will also be given to an assessment of the present state of the nation's health. We will then look to the health service changes and consider some aspects which may or may not provide us with the framework to carry out health promotional activities. An examination of the *Health of the Nation* strategy also will help to clarify the Government's own perspective on health, elucidate the expected role of the nurse, and indeed highlight the intended role for the NHS in the health promotional field. Firstly then, we will try to define what health may mean, so that we have some conceptual basis on which to progress this discussion.

What is health?

Definitions of the concept of health are wide-ranging, multifaceted and personal. Health may be viewed as absence of disease on one hand, as well-being on the other, or even something involving personal capacity or resources for living (Cribb, 1993).

Many terms also are used to denote something other than health: ill-health, sickness, disease, illness, disability, handicap, impairment. The multiple foci of writing and research about health and illness clearly reflect the different and differing perceptions held by professionals, politicians and the public alike.

The medical model

The dominant health model which has been powerfully supported over time is that created by the medical profession. This is unsurprising as they have been seen as the perceived experts on health and health care because of their greater knowledge and skills than other professionals.

> Stereotypically, the medical model can be viewed as thinking of man as a machine. Man is healthy when the human is in perfect working order, thus the engineering model. By tinkering around with the individual pieces (organs) the machine (man) can be repaired to function appropriately (Long, 1984).

Important parts of this model are that ill-health is seen as a natural and biological breakdown of the body, and, as ill-health befalls individuals, it is they who need to be cured or given care. It is unsurprising then that people have likened the NHS to 'a garage for putting faulty human bodies back on the road again' (Klein, 1992).

The wider environmental determinants of ill-health or health for that matter are not a consideration. The focus of diagnosis and cure is on the disease and its process, and so for example, surgery will be used to remove a cancer or drugs prescribed to relieve depression. Other wider health promotional activity around these would be beyond the medical model remit, so thus limiting or even ignoring the finding or eradication of the social root causes.

The social model of health

An opposing perception of health is one that views it as a concept with social origins. It has been referred to as having an ecological or environmental basis. It is demonstrated via the new public health approach of recent years, and is concerned with the wider determinants of health – life-styles, health services, economic policies and unemployment. As Goodwin explains:

> Like the 'old' public health, expounded by people like Florence Nightingale, and her Victorian medical officer of health contemporaries, the new public health is about environmental and personal health protection. But it goes much further to call for explicit public policies which will as the World Health Organisation puts it, make the healthy choices of behaviour and life-styles the easier choices (Goodwin, 1992).

Many as we all know have argued that greater levels of health and wellness are a result of better standards of living, and not necessarily because of our nursing and medical health services.

> The appraisal of influences on health in the past suggests that we owe the improvement, not to what happens when we are ill, but to the fact that we do not often become ill, and we remain well, not because of specific measures such as vaccination and immunisation, but because we enjoy a higher standard of nutrition and live in a healthier environment (McKeown, 1976).

The social model of health thus pushes attention and activity towards an emphasis on finding out why ill-health occurs, a greater concern for care over cure, and a shift towards an environmental or public health approach.

A nurse model for health?

Nurses in reality may well use a mix of the above health models as their guiding philosophy for care, perhaps stressing one side more than another depending upon their role and situation. In any event, it would be invidious and mechanistic to carve out one position or another in holy writ. Individuals need to reflect on their own philosophy of health and equate it to professional and contextual remits, with a good understanding of the real health issues faced by the population. As Cribb says:

> We cannot solve the problems of health care by fastening upon a definition of health. Some of the time it is helpful to use a conception of health which concentrates on specific measurable objectives; some of the time it is helpful to be reminded of the infinite variety of elements that can contribute to life's quality; and it is always helpful to remember that health care involves enabling individuals to function well as people and not just as biological organisms (Cribb, 1993).

In nursing education a commonly used definition of health over many years has been that of the World Health Organization in 1946 – a state of complete physical, mental and social well-being, not merely the absence of disease or infirmity (WHO, 1946). However, this has been criticized because it describes an ideal state which is unrealistic.

Others now look to perhaps more acceptable definitions of health which offer us some sort of realizable objective. We might consider that of the Ottawa Charter for Health (WHO, 1986b).

> Health is created and lived by people within the settings of their everyday life; where they learn, work, play and love. Health is created by caring for oneself and others, by being able to take decisions and have control over one's life circumstances, and by ensuring that the society one lives in

creates conditions that allow the attainment of health by all its members.

This definition is wide-ranging, embracing not only prevention of ill-health, but the promotion of health. It clearly represents 'an attempt to move from planning medical care services to planning for healthy people and healthy environments' (Luker and Orr, 1992). This perspective on health is in line with the goal of the World Health Organization of health for all by the year 2000 (WHO, 1978; WHO, 1981; WHO 1985):

> The main social target of WHO in the coming decades should be the attainment by all citizens of the world by the year 2000 of a level of health that will permit them to lead a socially and economically productive life.

The UK Government was a signatory to the 1984 agreement to work towards the *38 Health for All* targets set out for countries in the European region of WHO (WHO, 1984; WHO, 1986a). It is worth noting at this point that the Health Secretary, Virginia Bottomley, said she viewed the *Health of the Nation* strategy as keeping in line with WHO's aims and objectives. She said that these would be built on 'in a way designed to meet the particular circumstances in this country' (Department of Health, 1992a). Presumably she was linking the health strategy with that of the NHS reforms and wider Government and social and economic policy.

A healthy future for health promotion?

At this point then, we might conclude that the Government's strategy for both health provision and the NHS reforms reflect a definition of health, and thus a wide-ranging goal, aimed at all levels of intervention – primary, secondary and tertiary. It appears to offer nurses of whatever background the potential to develop their roles to ensure 'further continuing improvements in the health of the nation', and 'to provide even better health care for the millions and millions of people who rely on the National Health Service.'

If we now make some assessment of the health needs of the UK population as we approach the twenty-first century, perhaps then we will be better able to judge whether the newly reformed NHS is fit to meet these needs, or can only be expected to cope with some of them. We must also ask if the role of nursing is likely to be enlarged and enriched in what appears to be a new vision and emphasis by the Government on promoting the health of the nation.

How well is the nation now?

According to the health strategy White Paper 'health in England is better than it has ever been', and also to the Chief Medical Officer of Health, 'impressive changes in health have occurred since the first Public Health Report in 1858 and will continue to do so' (Department of Health, 1992b). Life expectancy at birth has increased vastly, maternal deaths in child birth have been reduced, infant mortality is down and death rates from infectious diseases have fallen drastically. However, whilst all this is good news, the ever-developing pattern of health and illness in the UK means that new, modern, complex health agendas have developed which need to be addressed urgently. For example, we might think of the emergence of human immunodeficiency virus (HIV) and acquired immunodeficiency syndrome (AIDS), the developments in genetic engineering and the many surrounding ethical debates, the advances in medical technology and the potential for the prolongation of life, the impact of an ageing population, and all the challenges which accompany this important demographic transition.

In addition to all of this, and in spite of the many acknowledged improvements and ongoing effort, 'there are still areas where Britain's health record compares badly with other western nations. Most countries have been more successful at reducing the rate of premature death from coronary heart disease' (Pike, 1991).

It is of little surprise then to see that coronary heart disease and strokes are amongst the key areas highlighted for action in the health strategy paper, which also includes related cancers, mental illness, HIV infection and AIDS, sexual health and accidents. It is acknowledged that in spite of greater longevity, many people still die before they reach the age of 65, or have their lives impaired by the effects of ill-health. It is argued also that this could be avoided if individuals changed their life-styles and health behaviours.

Others of course would look not 'just to a change in individual health behaviour, but more significantly to social and environmental changes to alleviate some of the root causes of health problems and to provide an equality of opportunity for optimum health' (Cork, 1990).

If as nurses we claim to have an eclectic view of the determinants of health, then any assessment of the nation's health surely must be mindful of the greatly increased levels of unemployment in the past decade, the well-reported increasing gap between top and bottom income groups and the greater incidence of relative poverty and homelessness (Mason, 1993). These are without doubt impinging upon the potential health and well-being of large numbers of the population. If any *Health for All* programme is to be realized for *all* rather than for *some*, then any strategies for health and health care services will by definition need to be wide-ranging, show flair and imagination and be backed by resources. The question then becomes whether or not the new NHS is now able, or indeed was ever intended to be involved in such a challenge for the future. The answer to this question is vitally important for nurses as they seek to clarify their roles in the ever changing NHS work environment. Let us first think about the shape and remit of the old-style NHS.

The NHS 1948–1989 – health or illness promoter?

All Governments have been quick to acknowledge the virtues of the NHS, whilst simultaneously pruning and changing parts of its organization and structure as the years have passed. However, in spite of its contribution to upholding the nation's health, public health measures have surely also contributed to a great extent. Indeed, the World Health Organization has said:

> The key to solving many health problems lies outside the health sector or is in the hands of people themselves – in order to meet contemporary challenges to health, it is necessary for all elements of society to contribute.

They look to health authorities, local authorities, primary health care sectors, health education authorities, voluntary sector, industry and the media to play their part.

To develop this line of discussion of course might be construed as an argument to disestablish the NHS as our main state-run health provider organization. This would be scarcely a tenable conclusion, because the intent is to present an argument that if we do acknowledge a wide concept of health as our goal for action, then we need to understand that health care needs are clearly met by a wide range of NHS and non-NHS people and organizations. The NHS has never, and could never alone meet such a challenge. What *has* happened though, is that stress has been laid, and continues to be laid, on secondary and tertiary interventions at the expense of primary health care. As such, the NHS is not surprisingly, perceived by many as an illness service, or as noted earlier, as 'a garage for putting faulty human bodies back on the road again.' The promotion of health appears as a sideline in the business of health care provision.

In response to such an accusation the Government might well refer us back to the White Paper *Promoting Better Health* (Department of Health, 1987), to the new GP contract (Department of Health and the Welsh Office, 1989) and to their support for a health focused nurse education programme in Project 2000 (UKCC, 1986). Nonetheless, high-tech medical interventions in a hospital setting have, over time, been perceived by the public, health professionals and politicians alike as evidence and proof of a successful health service, fit for a highly developed society and nation. Forty years of NHS policy which have reflected this stance, have left a structure, organization and a culture within the NHS which still reflects old roots that are illness-based and focused on medicine. So do we have something different in the newly created NHS?

The NHS post-1989 – illness or health promoter?

The Government's review of the fault strewn old NHS was perceived by many as an examination of only one part of the total health care picture in the UK. By definition, how could it be anything else? The assessment of the NHS and its workings was not concerned with exploring the potential of the ongoing wider fringe health care activity, least of all that which blurred with what was to be termed 'social care' and social issues. The review was about hospitals, general practice and ill people, and not about a positive health agenda and all that this implies. In this way, the review only provided at best a partial diagnosis and thus a partial prescription for improving health care provision. It really cannot be seen as even trying to meet the wide and complex health care issues of UK society today. As Harrison *et al.* (1989) said, 'The diagnosis it can be argued, is rather narrow and pays scant regard to wider issues including the persistence of health inequalities, the level of preventable illness, and alleged underfunding of the NHS which prompted the review in the first place.' Others have argued that the White Paper continued 'to see the NHS as a national hospital service with its title – *Working For Patients* – reflecting a lack of commitment to health promotion and preventive medicine' (Community Outlook, 1989).

Goodwin believed the White Paper was not 'much interested in health as such; health promotion is only mentioned once in passing as one of the responsibilities of health authorities, with no clue as to how that responsibility will be expressed in service terms' (Goodwin, 1989b).

The Association of Community Health Councils (ACHCEW, 1989) noted that the White Paper was orientated almost entirely to the acute sector, and that huge sections of the NHS were omitted or dealt with cursorily. Community care was not discussed, and public health referred to only briefly.

The RCN said the Government in its review 'was looking up the wrong end of a telescope, and should be concentrating its attention not on acute care, but on services for the large and rising numbers of elderly people and on the promotion of good health' (Editorial, *Nursing Times*, 1989).

Grave doubts were expressed early on as to the review's findings and solutions. Not only in more general terms was the document perceived as lacking in detail concerning the proposed changes, and as a threat to the long-term viability of the principles underlying a national health service – but it appeared isolationist in its exclusivity of emphasis on hospital and medical services. It also presented a limited view of the concept of health and the role of nurses (particularly community nurses) who would have expected to be mentioned more widely.

Community nurses' concerns

The continuing emphasis on the medical and curative aspects, is exemplified by the persistent support of the model for health care for people outside hospital which concentrates on the GP as first point of contact. This is totally in line of course with the trend of general practice empowerment and development following the 1987 White Paper (Fatchett, 1989; Fatchett, 1990). The opportunity for community nurses to take a different and truly primary health care approach to care as proposed in the Cumberlege Report (Department of Health and Social Security, 1986) was rejected by the Government. With the GP as first point of contact health interventions invariably become secondary and tertiary. Others of course will disagree, looking to the health promotional aspects of the GP contract. In order to show that positive health approaches are indeed supported they look to those nurses in general practice who they claim, now have unlimited opportunity for enormous creativity in their primary health care role. Health visitors, district nurses and many others also, similarly carry out a wide variety of well-reported health promotional activity on behalf of health authorities.

However, if community nurses are so important in delivering the Government's positive health strategy why did they only merit a single line in the White Paper? District nurses and health visitors (and what about all the other community nurses?) were seen as needed to be provided locally 'on grounds of practicality' and health promotion was only referred to in passing as one of the responsibilities of health authorities. So much then for acknowledgement of the enormous amount of effective primary health care work that has been, and is being carried out by nurses in the community. One might be forgiven for describing it as dismissive.

Health – social care split

Another concern expressed at the time of publication of the White Paper, was that no response or reference to the Griffiths' Report on Community Care (Griffiths, 1988) was made. Accusations flew around, and dismay was expressed because the NHS appeared to be equated with hospital services and general practice. The total focus appeared to be on illness and treatment, and other levels of caring and states of wellness were ignored. Large groups in the population (e.g. the elderly, the mentally handicapped, the disabled) appeared to be off the agenda, but who clearly do receive care from the NHS nurses and other professionals. No true positive health agenda was addressed because presumably it was not seen as NHS business. Both health care and health appeared to be defined tightly (although no explicit definitions were given), and effectively the role of nurses was made leaner. Indeed, the publication of the Government's Community Care White Paper, *Caring for People* (Department of Health, 1989c) only confirmed fears that health care was indeed being redefined and its remit slimmed down. Social care was to become the responsibility of local authorities and social carers.

It is little wonder then that community nurses in particular began to express discomfort at this stage, not only for their professional survival, but as health promoters concerned with the multiplicity of determinants of health. They felt their activities were being compromised and potential role enrichment disappearing. The unnatural split being created between health (health authority) and social care (local authority) concerns appeared to challenge their holistic nursing approach to work. Their employing health authorities, with an eye on budgets, were very likely to define how far their work could merge and cross with local authority provision.

Indeed, the expressed wish of the Government to ensure that 'nurses' time is deployed to best effect on work which requires special skills, leaving work which does not require those skills to be done by others' reflects, as we will see in the next chapter, the early dissection and paring down of the professional role of the nurse by others; others who fail to understand that nursing care is about much more than providing technical skills and acting as assistants to doctors. Nurses are concerned with all the realities of people's lives not just those tasks which can be easily qualified, quantified and costed. Unfortunately the changes presented in both the NHS and community care reform White Papers reinforce a medicalised concept of health and health care, and this underpins what the role of the nurse will be within the NHS. This will in turn serve to create in reality a fragmentation of care by the nurse and perhaps a reduction in standards for those who receive that care.

Fragmentation or integration of care?

It is worth noting that health policy analysts have described the creation of this organizational split in delivering health and social care as a profound turning point in NHS history. According to Holliday (1992) the earlier 1974 NHS reorganization was a change based on a theme of organizational integration, bringing together those strands of health care provision which had been split in a tripartite fashion in 1948 when the NHS began. The aim in 1974 was to bring together primary, hospital and community care services to improve health care planning and organization and thus to improve further the nation's health.

It is somewhat strange then to see a new 1990 fragmentation of care provision with the emergence of hospital and community trusts, directly managed units, budget holding practices, new local authority responsibilities, and the increasing promotion of private and voluntary sector involvement. In effect, the new health and social care internal market structures have surely created fragmented rather than integrated means of meeting the health needs of the population. Whether or not this will provide the smooth and seamless care so promised, is debatable. However, if we doubt the method and process set up to promote the nation's health, we must accept a potential threat to achieving healthy outcomes.

> For patients and clients . . . the threat can be simply stated –
> the major risk for them lies in the inevitable fragmentation of
> care into easy-to-cost units which bear no relationship to the
> continuity of human lives, in sickness or in health (Goodwin,
> 1989a).

So far then we have observed the apparent focus of the health reforms on the hospital and medical services, coupled with the virtual disregard for community care, and the limited mention of public health. Sadly, this perhaps represents a belief that they are not aspects central to health care provision, or indeed to the conceptual framework for health promotion embodied within NHS provision. The apparent emphasis appears to be on directing resources to services for ill people rather than at health promotional activity. In response to that final accusation, however, others will refer us to the promising remit for the District Health Authorities. As the White Paper said:

> DHAs can . . . concentrate on ensuring that the health needs
> of the population for which they are responsible are met; that

there are effective services for the prevention and control of diseases and the promotion of health; that their population has access to a comprehensive range of high quality, value for money services (Department of Health, 1989a).

All of the above does sound an optimistic note. However, we need to reflect on the fact that no definitions of either 'health' or 'need' are provided in the White Paper, and thus the purpose of the NHS in general, and DHAs in this particular instance are unclear and ill-defined.

The DHAs of course could take the opportunity to tackle persistent environmentally and socially induced health problems in their authority areas, and thus provide a very welcome response. They could also wear their strictly 'market hats' and pursue narrow non-risk taking approaches with an eye to budget balances and contract making. In light of experience at this stage, it would seem that the latter scenario is more likely. DHAs like local authorities implementing community care reforms have had to bow to the realities of resources available both in terms of finance and services when making assessments of need. Cost conscious purchasers cannot afford to take risks when their own employment contracts are on the line, and so the temptation is surely to take the well-trodden paths of mainstream health care activity. It has always been easier to quantify physical/medical interventions than to measure activities with potentially unmeasurable outcomes. You only have to ask any health visitor about some of their resourcing difficulties for health education and promotion, in particular with work concerned with the homeless, travellers, prostitutes, indeed in any less than mainstream health care fields.

At this point we might conclude that the NHS review and subsequent Act have created new market-like structures, businesslike aims and objectives, and further reinforced the

limited medicalized concept of health which has under-
pinned much NHS activity over time. Far from opening up
into the wider fields of social and environmental health, the
NHS appeared to be pulled back even more than ever into a
medical and illness service. Whilst some of the descriptive
language in the White Paper emphasized the opposite, the
detail within it, and the subsequent Working Papers
(Department of Health, 1989b) probably provide a truer
picture of policy intentions. Doctors, medical services and
hospitals were placed centre stage, and nurses essentially
ignored. Within the NHS, nurses as health promoters would
be potentially limited in those aspects which would be perceived as within their health care remits. It is against this
particular backcloth that the *Health of the Nation* strategy
must be examined. It seems already impossible to imagine
that the newly emerging NHS will be in any way fit enough
to meet that particular role.

The Health of the Nation – the Green Paper (Department of Health, 1991)

Having introduced its controversial health service reforms,
the Government according to many critics, published its
Green Paper on health to divert attention towards more
positive discussion. According to William Waldegrave
(Secretary of State for Health) it was:

> The first time that an explicit health strategy has been pro-
> posed for England. At its heart is the proposal to set chal-
> lenging health objectives and targets to improve the overall
> health of the nation. Their scope reflects the fact that my task
> as Secretary of State is to focus on better health just as much
> as better health care. The Green Paper enshrines that wider
> health objective. I am happy to tell the House that our
> approach has been endorsed in warm terms by the World

Health Organization whose *Health For All by the year 2000*
programme started the production of such strategies worldwide (Waldegrave, 1991a).

So whilst the earlier reforms laid emphasis on mechanisms, and means rather than ends, attention was now to be
focused on improvements in health. A very consensual
approach appeared to be taken by involving and inviting as
much opinion as possible to discuss the paper's contents,
unlike in the case of the NHS Review. However, criticism
still came.

Many were pleased to see an acknowledgement of the
multiplicity of determinants of health 'from genetic inheri-
tance, through personal behaviour, family and social circumstances to the physical and social environment'
(Delamothe, 1991).

But for others, the Green Paper failed to recognize the
importance of poverty as a cause of poor health and to rec-
ommend targets for its reduction (Carlisle, 1991b; Hodges,
1991). It failed to see the importance of unemployment and
poor housing. It did not address the issue of health inequalities. It lacked a commitment to sufficient funding.
Insufficient weight was placed on the role of government
departments other than the Department of Health. Indeed
doubts were expressed as to the commitment of the
Government as a whole. It was also seen as placing too
much emphasis on the role of individual action and not
enough on collective action.

Clearly, there were supporters who viewed it as a potential opportunity for the NHS to be moved towards a new
health agenda rather than remaining an illness focused service. Others in response expressed more cynical feelings as
to the Government's true intentions. Having felt profoundly
challenged by the NHS review, and being somewhat unbe-
lieving as to the promises about the necessary level of

resourcing for the NHS, it was clearly hard for some to believe that the Government was taking the health agenda seriously. It did little to reassure sceptics that on the very day that the Green Paper was launched in the House of Commons, Conservative MEPs were vetoing a proposed ban on tobacco advertizing throughout Europe (Carlisle, 1991b). So, whilst on one hand demonstrating some awareness of the need for a collective response by Government in promoting the people's health, it failed to follow through some of its own ideas and it provided a partial response only. For example, as one commentator said:

the food safety and diet targets do not extend to changing government policy nutritional guidelines for schools or for an integrated food and agriculture policy. They ignore the clear evidence that the difference in income between the rich and poor is the major determinant of a nation's health. Instead the targets are centred around individual behaviour and specific disease (Scott-Samuel in Carlisle, 1991).

It was inevitable, and perhaps understandable, that many in the nursing and medical media criticized the contents fully.

The Health of the Nation – White Paper 1992

The publication of the White Paper response in July 1992 was slightly delayed because of the intervening April General Election. The White Paper was, according to Virginia Bottomley, a landmark for the NHS and the next logical step in health care reforms. As she explained:

It was to provide us with new opportunities to raise our sights beyond the provision of health care – important though that is – to health itself. The National Health Service was to be at the centre of that strategy, but other organisations, every department in Whitehall, private companies and voluntary bodies, local authorities, health authorities, employers, trade unions, and individuals of every age would need to play their part (Department of Health, 1992a).

Many commentators welcomed the new stress on promoting health, and although acknowledging the obvious importance of working at the five selected areas for action, were disappointed that the emphasis was on preventing specific illnesses rather than promoting health. Again, and unsurprisingly, great concern was expressed at the failure to address the issues of poverty, inequality, unemployment and poor housing. As one said, 'The Government has set simplistic targets, but they do not address the underlying issues. Poverty and deprivation are important factors in ill-health. Mrs. Bottomley has floated a few ideas but you could hardly call it a strategy – it's largely window dressing' (Kearney in Mihill, 1992).

The HVA for example pointed out that studies clearly demonstrated links between poverty and children's health, and Buttigieg expressed her fears that 'it was hard to see how this White Paper will bring real help to families struggling to raise healthy children in substandard housing with barely enough money to feed them through the week' (Buttigieg, 1992).

Other criticisms included the document's emphasis on individual as opposed to collective action, and with this, a lack of belief that sufficient funding would be forthcoming to carry out the work needed as, 'the intention is to focus resources' already given to the NHS (Carlisle, 1992).

One issue which pervaded much of the White Paper discussion is that of smoking and the lack of a ban on tobacco advertising. As Chambers *et al* (1991) had pointed out the year before, 'Glamorous images of smoking portrayed by the industry undermine the influence of health education in schools, and help to create the view that smoking is adult and socially acceptable. If the Government is serious about achieving the smoking targets and protecting children from the promotion of cigarettes it should support a ban.'

To date the Government is still relying on price, education, self-control, and a review of the role of advertizing as a means of achieving their health targets on smoking. They have refused to support European Community proposals for a ban. In a reply to Liz Lynne MP in July 1992 concerning this point, Virginia Bottomley said it was hard 'to take lessons from countries whose records in the reduction of smoking leaves much to be desired' (Bottomley, 1992). It might be suggested that a less confrontational response to our European partners would be more helpful if the Government wish to convince would-be supporters of their seriousness about promoting health. As it is, this sort of indifference, and general lack of preparedness to listen to health professionals and others must surely be of concern. They have claimed to listen and act on what they hear:

> We are clear about one thing: a strategy imposed by Government which takes no need of the views of those who will have to implement it, including the people themselves, is valueless (Smith, 1991).

However, their responses elsewhere cast doubt on their listening skills, and perhaps demonstrate the paucity of their promises.

Perhaps then, some nurses might well reflect on their experience so far and wonder if they have been involved in any broader promotion of health. The NHS changes appear to have laid emphasis on medical–illness aspects of care. The concept of health underpinning both nursing activity and thus health promotion has been reduced. The health promotion strategy outlined in the White Paper chose targets which were illness focused, and appeared to off-load the responsibility of controlling the social determinants of health on to others – many of whom do not work within the NHS umbrella. Whilst accepting that health promotion activity indeed belongs to many other arenas also, the *Health of the Nation* strategy can never bring the improvements it says it wants without a commitment from all other government departments to tackle the wider issues of poverty and poor housing.

> To make real progress we need an economy based on employment, proper childcare, good housing and support for single parents. In the end those are the gaps in the Health of the Nation (Buttigieg in Mason, 1993).

If we consider all the activity now in hand to reduce still further the welfare state provision derived from invalidity and other benefits, and the persistence of high unemployment, it is easy to see that many individuals are probably finding it more and more difficult to take decisions and have control over life circumstances. A large group of the population are now needing to be 'helped to health' more than ever before, and sadly the strategy being followed for the NHS appears to be limited. Other government departments we know are looking to control their own budgets, and are highly unlikely to want to pick up the bill for another department's bright idea. The situation is obviously unclear, and it would seem that the health strategy is potentially a mere sideshow to the wider changes taking place in the NHS.

Where are we now?

At the beginning of this discussion we questioned whether or not the new NHS changes would hinder or promote the carrying out of the health strategy. On balance, the jury is still out on these questions, although early evidence would cast doubt upon the argument that the NHS reforms will lead to a coherent and effective health strategy. Nurses meanwhile should take up all opportunities to build 'healthy alliances' with other non-NHS agencies, and try to take up the responsibility of creating healthier and safer environments. They should collect evidence of need and use this to negotiate seriously for NHS resources to both widen the remit, and increase the potential for health promotional activity, within what appears to be a more limited medicalized NHS framework.

References

Acheson Donald (1988) *Foreword. Public Health In England*. Cmd. 289. London, HMSO.

ACHCEW (Association of Community Health Councils) (1989) *Working for Patients? – Response To The Government's Review Of The NHS*. Draft 5.

Beveridge William (1942) *Social Insurance And Allied Services*. Cmd. 6404.

Black Sir Douglas (1980) *Inequalities in Health: Report of A Research Working Group*. London, HMSO.

Bottomley Virginia MP (1992) *Statement On The Health Of The Nation White Paper*. H. C. Debate; c.335. Hansard.

Buttigieg Margaret in Turner T (1992) A healthy nation. *Nursing Times*, **88**(30).

Buttigieg Margaret in Mason P (1993) Healthy living. *Nursing Times*, **89**(11).

Carlisle Daloni (1991a) Minister spells out targets for health. *Nursing Times*, **87**(24).

Carlisle Daloni (1991b) Planning the future. *Nursing Times*, **87**(27).

Carlisle Daloni (1992) Profession is key to white paper goals. *Nursing Times*, **88**(29).

Chambers Jacky, Killoran A and McNeill A (1991) Smoking. *British Medical Journal*, **303:** 973–977.

Community Outlook (1989) *Hidden opportunities*. March.

Cork Morwenna (1990) Approaches to health promotion. *Midwife, Health Visitor and Community Nurse*, **26**(5).

Cribb A (1993) in Hinchliff S., Norman S. and Schober J. (eds) *Nursing Practice and Health Care, 2nd edn*. London, Edward Arnold.

Delamothe Tony (1991) Health manifestos: the Government. *British Medical Journal*, **302**, 1355–56.

Department of Health and Social Security (1986) *Neighbourhood Nursing – A Focus for Care* (Cumberlege Report). London, HMSO.

Department of Health (1987) *Promoting Better Health*. Cmd. 249. London, HMSO.

Department of Health (1989a) *Working For Patients*. Cmd. 555. London, HMSO.

Department of Health (1989b) *National Health Service Review Working Papers*. (Package of 8 booklets). London, HMSO.

Department of Health (1989c) *Caring For People*. Cmd. 849. London, HMSO.

Department of Health and the Welsh Office (1989) *General Practice In The National Health Service. A New Contract*. London, HMSO.

Department of Health (1991) *The Health Of The Nation: A Consultative Document For Health In England*. Cmd. 1523. London, HMSO.

Department of Health (1992a) *The Health Of The Nation*. Cmd. 1986. London, HMSO.

Department of Health (1992b) *On The State Of The Public Health 1991*. London, HMSO.

Editorial (Nursing Times) (1989) *Nursing Times*, **85** (12).

Fatchett Anita (1989) Going the way of the dinosaur? *Nursing Times*, **85**(27).

Fatchett Anita (1990) Health visiting: a withering profession? *Journal of Advanced Nursing* **15**, 216–22.

Foot Michael (1973) *Aneurin Bevan* Vol. 2. London, Davis Poynter.

Goodwin Shirley (1989a) Storm clouds ahead? *Nursing Times*, **85**(10).

Goodwin Shirley (1989b) Looking between the lines of the white paper. *Health Visitor*, **62**.

Goodwin Shirley (1992) Community nursing and the new public health. *Health Visitor*, **65**(3).

Griffiths Roy (1988) *Community Care: Agenda For Action*. London, HMSO.

Harrison Steve, Hunter David, Johnston Ian and Wistow Gerald (1989) Competing for health. *A Commentary on the NHS Review*. Nuffield Institute Reports, University of Leeds.

Hodges Catharine (1991) Health of the nation. *Nursing Times*, **87**(48).

Holliday Ian (1992) *The NHS Transformed*. Manchester, Baseline Books.

Kearney in Mihill C. (1992) Strategy for improvement or window-dressing. *The Guardian*, July 9.

Klein Rudolph (1992) Strengths and frailities of the 1942 citizen's charter. *The Guardian*, March 4.

Long A (1984) *Research into Health and Illness*. London, Gower.

Luker K and Orr J (1992) *Towards Community Health Nursing*. Oxford, Blackwell Scientific Publications.

Mason Peter (1993) Healthy living. *Nursing Times*, **89**(11).

McKeown T (1976) *The Role Of Medicine: Dream, Mirage or Nemesis?* Nuffield Provincial Hospitals Trust. Oxford, Oxford University Press.

Pike A (1991) A delicate operation. *Financial Times*, March 28.

Scott-Samuel, A. (1991) in Carlisle Daloni, 'Planning the Future', *Nursing Times* **87**(27).

Smith Richard (1991) First steps towards a strategy for health. *British Medical Journal*, **303**, 297–299.

United Kingdom Central Council (1986) *Project 2000: A New Preparation For Practice*. London, UKCC.

Waldegrave William MP (1991a) *Statement On The Health Of The Nation Consultative Document*. H.C. Debate; C.155. Hansard.

World Health Organization (1946) *Constitution*. Geneva, WHO.

World Health Organization (1978) *Primary Health Care*. Geneva, WHO.

World Health Organization (1981) *Global Strategy For Health For All By The Year 2000*. Geneva, WHO.

World Health Organization (1984) *Regional Strategy For Health For All By The Year 2000*. Geneva, WHO.

World Health Organization (1985) Targets For Health For All. Copenhagen, WHO.

World Health Organization (1986a) *Nursing And The 38 Targets Of Health For All – A Discussion Paper*. Nursing Unit, Copenhagen, WHO/Euro.

World Health Organization (1986b) *Ottawa Charter For Health Promotion*. Canadian Public Health Association, Copenhagen WHO/Euro.

5

Nurses and the NHS

Nurses have faced tremendous upheavals in the NHS over the past decade, caused by a combination of managerial, technological, political, economic and social changes. These have contributed to, and culminated in, the imposition of general management on the NHS, and a more commercialized approach (Griffiths, 1983), and also, the implementation of the NHS reforms (Department of Health, 1989) with its internal health care market mechanisms. Since 1 April 1991, and the start of the changes, few nurses will be unaware of the challenges posed by these reforms to the role of the nurse and to associated professional values.

In very practical terms, the golden age of certainty about long term careers in, and general support for nursing as a developing profession appears to be under threat from the new NHS culture. The values underpinning a market approach to health care distribution will by definition relate directly to the measurement of costs and money flows, rather than to the vaguer, peripheral qualitative concepts around service to the client or indeed for this discussion, to support for nurse professional growth and development. As Mangan describes it:

> The jobs of many nurse practitioners, managers and teachers are coming under threat as organisations increasingly question their effectiveness, and search for an increasing number of ways of saving money (Mangan, 1993).

Recent years have been particularly threatening ones, with unsatisfactory pay awards, the introduction of skill–mix reviews, and job cuts. Doubts have been expressed by one Professor of Health Service Management, Eric Caines, as to the need to maintain existing levels of qualified nurses in employment because support workers could do much of their work (Caines, 1993; Snell, 1993). Indeed, according to another influential Professor of Health Management, Roger Dyson, student nurse intakes should be frozen in some parts of the country, and tutors freed to work in wards. He also argued that registered nurses are overtrained to care for patients in clinical settings, and that nurses should show more flexibility by working and moving between any surgical or medical speciality as staffing level necessity dictates (Downey, 1993). It is of no surprise that these controversial views have been angrily refuted by many nurse academics, practitioners and their professional representatives.

Jane Robinson, Professor of Nursing at Nottingham University has challenged Eric Caines (formerly in NHS management) to come up with the evidence for his claims, reminding him that he was no longer in the political arena, but in academia where you need to back up what you say with hard evidence (Robinson in Snell, 1993). Christine Hancock, RCN General Secretary, has also questioned his claims. She has referred on many occasions to studies showing that qualified nurses not surprisingly help patients to get better faster, and that patients wanted all round nursing care (Hancock, 1993). Hector MacKenzie, COHSE General Secretary, has reminded Caines also that staffing in the NHS is not the same as running a supermarket, and that no one with any experience of health work could seriously believe that cutting 20% of trained staff would improve patient care (Snell, 1993a).

As for Professor Dyson's opinions as to the acceptability

of ward sisters being sent to work in either medical or surgical wards depending upon required staffing demands, Betty Kershaw (Principal of Stockport, Tameside and Glossop College of Nursing), viewed these ideas 'with absolute disgust'. She reminded the audience of ward sisters at the conference both she and Dyson were addressing: 'Doctors are not asked to do this, so why should nurses?' (Downey, 1993).

We will return to this question a little later in our discussion and try to find out why overtime nurses do seem to have had a weaker claim to professional status and power than, for example, the doctors. We will also consider why NHS managers and those who are otherwise concerned with managerial issues, appear to view nurses as the softer target for implementing changes in both activity and numbers employed within the NHS today.

The NHS reforms: A challenge to nurses as professionals

Sadly, it does appear that the role of the nurse, and the associated professional values and achievements are being questioned now that the NHS reforms are underway. Perhaps we should really feel little surprise at such an outcome. After all, claims and practice have not always gone hand in hand following the reforms. In earlier chapters for instance, it has been argued that the creation of an internal health care market and increased commercialization of NHS activities have not necessarily improved the service for all. Health care consumers are not intrinsically being further empowered, but offered some sort of 'window dressing' of choice. The avowed intent to make the NHS more concerned with the promotion of good health is also questionable because of the reforms' emphasis on secondary care. Flaws and cracks have appeared in the newly emerging NHS market environment which have created uncertainties and inequalities in provision, which feel sharper and more uncomfortable than they ever did before the changes took place.

Nurses are central players in the evolving new style NHS by virtue of their sheer numbers in the workforce, and because of their integral part in providing health care. (Robinson K in Robinson J *et al.* (eds), 1992). They cannot be above or removed from the perverse outcomes already noted, and as such, the impact of the managerial and market culture within the NHS must also be controlling the extent to which nurse professional development can be encouraged and afforded. It is clear that high status professionals will be expensive to employ in great numbers, and the creation or maintenance of a more flexible, less powerful and cheaper workforce must hold an obvious appeal to cost conscious managers. It is around such ideas that this chapter will develop.

The following discussion will attempt to examine the impact of the Government's strategy for the NHS on the professional role and values of nursing. A number of questions will be addressed:

1 What is a professional?
2 How has nursing's professional role developed over time?
3 What have been the effects of Government health policy on the professional role of the nurse?
4 What has been the impact of the NHS reforms on the nursing profession?

Some answers to these will help to clarify what is happening to nursing. So firstly then, the concept of a professional will be examined.

What is a professional?

In very common usage the term professional is seen as a collective symbol of high value (Becker, 1970), often implying dedication and commitment. However, from the vast expanse of literature on it, there emerges a multitude of definitions and perspectives (see Hugman, 1991; Turner, 1991). The analysis of the concept of a professional has been a major pre-occupation of sociologists over time (see for example, Durkheim, 1951; Weber, 1966; Parsons, 1939; Freidson, 1970; Johnson, 1972). It is evident that like any discussion around the concept of health, for example, the debates around the nature of a professional are also complex, sometimes contradictory, and in the end rely upon individual perception, understanding and experience. A brief note however on just some of the points raised will help to clarify the discussions to follow.

Durkheim (1951), for example looked to the professional groups as representing an institutionalization of personal service and community welfare. Weber (1966) described professionals as motivated by neither personal interests nor economic reward. Parsons (1939, 1951) emphasized the ethical nature of their work, providing a service to others based on technical knowledge. Mannheim described them as providing a guarantee of objectivity and being above sectional interests (see Turner, 1991). Kaye in turn looked to a profession as 'an occupation possessing skilled intellectual technique, a voluntary association and a code of conduct.' He believed that the last factor, the code of conduct, provided 'the guarantee of integrity, that is the main distinguishing mark of the professions.' (Kaye in Prandy, 1965). This 'guarantee of integrity' will be referred to later when we examine the issue of whistleblowing and attempts to apply professional codes of conduct where standards of practice or care appear to be compromised in health care settings.

Meanwhile, other views on the nature of professions are also worthy of note. Greenwood (1957), and Millerson (1964) have listed characteristics or traits of professional groups, as follows:

- skills based on theoretical understanding;
- autonomy in judgements;
- tested competence in achieving prescribed standards; and
- possession of a service ethic, so that they work for the common good rather than in their own self interest.

As Hugman explains it:

> Each occupation to be considered as a candidate for the label professional could be compared to the list of traits, and the degree to which it matched was then taken as an indication of the extent to which the occupation was professional (Hugman, 1991).

Following from this Etzioni (1969) applied the 'trait' approach to nurses, social workers and teachers, and defined them as semi-professionals, because he found them to be highly managed and controlled within their working environments. In addition, their work he suggested, lacked specific (to them) theoretical underpinning and emphasized skills rather than knowledge. By comparison, medicine and law for example had a greater claim to professional status than nursing.

In yet another perspective, professionalism is seen as a form of occupational control (Friedson, 1970; Johnson, 1972). In this way the profession decides who should or should not belong, for instance, in nursing through the use of state registration. In this way a qualified nurse for example is acknowledged to be a safer and more knowledgeable practitioner than someone who is not. Such self-regulation is very common amongst health carers throughout the world (Peters *et al.* 1978). The specialist knowledge and skills acquired by members enable them to a greater or lesser degree to claim autonomy in judgements about their care, and to be free from management and supervision. In reality of course, the ability of any health care professional to wield total power or control over their work is constrained by others. This is likely to involve members of the same profession, other allied professions, those who are paying for the care, the consumers or users of the services, and wider social institutions, for example, acting on behalf of the Government. By these means, the content and activity of professional care in whatever sphere, is determined both within and without, and between professions. The power relationships thus created are obviously complex, with all sides seeking to achieve their own ends by both overt and covert means. Suffice it to say, all professional groups within the NHS have not been immune from such processes during their development.

Professionals in the NHS

The NHS is crammed with professionals. They would all to a greater or lesser degree subscribe to a traditional vision of their role: the notion of having operational autonomy, a concern with giving service immediately to a client in need, a belief that their specialist knowledge and skills can only be provided by members of their particular profession. Indeed, they must by definition see themselves as protecting the public from outsiders, for example, from unscrupulous practitioners who have been expelled from their professional body, from quacks, amateurs and unscientific methods. It is no wonder then that any group would wish to be acknowledged as a profession, and to have the opportunity to shape their practice and to garner good financial rewards in the process. According to Heller (1978) the medical profession could be said to have achieved such professional status and power within the NHS. Nurses, however, have clearly been less successful in this quest, and have failed to achieve control over their practice, with their autonomy and power clearly circumscribed by managerial hierarchies.

Nurses as professionals: debates and development over time

The debate around whether or not nurses are professionals is often hot and full of fury with one branch asserting its predominance of attributes over another. Whilst Watkins (1992) refers to health visiting and midwifery as professions, he states that nursing:

> lacks the key attributes of a profession, its members are not mutually supportive; they do not seek to control their own work, it does not have high expectations of its working conditions, its brightest and ablest members are not the ones who rise in it.

Another commentator McEvoy (1992), refers to 'nursing as not yet exhibiting the full characteristics of a profession, but as soundly established on the continuum.' He and others (see Bridges, 1991), note a variety of ways in which progress had been made for example with the creation of professional organizations, the development of an international code of ethics, the development of conceptual frameworks for practice, the creation of degree courses in nursing and the emergence of nursing research upon which to base practice.

In spite of such positive progress, Watkins notes 'the dead hand of nursing attitudes' which halt those who wish to make greater professional strides than others. In this context he cites those nurses who side with obstetricians against midwives who seek independent practitioner status. Whilst clearly not referring to this midwifery example, Rundell (1991) notes in a similar vein that: 'The nursing profession appears happy to defer to its "betters" to avoid its responsibilities, and readily defends the prejudices and bizarre rituals of its colleagues in medicine for the sake of a quiet life.' He believes that people in general, and nurses in particular, still defer to doctors instead of valuing nursing as a profession every bit as skilled and valuable as medicine. However, this is hardly surprising, because of the historical closeness of nursing to medicine. It is perhaps because of the long-time pursuit of, and adherence to the medical knowledge base and values, that nursing has failed to achieve the status and power as a distinct profession with its own theory base and *raison d'être*.

Another anti-professionalizing attitude amongst nurses is the commonly held belief that nurses have to be all things to all people to prove that they are good professionals. Surely, however, to develop as a profession, nursing needs good managers, good educators, good practitioners, good researchers, good politicians and good writers. Other professions would expect no less. As Watkins (1992) stated:

> Most professions advance their most able members: nurses treat colleagues who advance to the top as dysfunctional: a nurse who moves into management is either seen to have 'failed' as a nurse or as not a true nurse (see Faugier, 1992; Shelley, 1993).

Indeed, any nurse who tries to take a stand for nursing is often vilified and left standing alone, because occupational solidarity in nursing has been historically poor. Whilst doctors will support their own and have very powerful professional representative organizations, nurse organizations too often seem to be in competitive bidding for members on the one hand, whilst on the other, fiercely defending status

hierarchies in a way which makes it impossible to have col-
laboration with other groups of NHS employees (see
Murray, 1990 on the ambulance dispute; Cohen, 1993).
Sadly, these internal arguments may also be sapping important energies which could be used elsewhere to better effect
in the pursuit of professional role. It has been said that
nurses often fail to appreciate the power of wider societal
factors which determine the context within which nursing is
carried out, and which in turn define the status and content
of nurse work. According to Robinson (1991) the inequalities which are seen in society as a whole are reflected in the
nursing workforce. The exploitation of women in the wider
society is thus recreated in health care settings. As
Gamarnikow (1978) has explained,

> Women are exploited as nurses because they are socialised
> into a doctrine which associates nursing with mothering, and
> sees the hospital ward as merely an expansion of the domes-
> tic sphere of labour.

In this way 'the good women' (Nightingale, 1881) or
'housewives of medicine' (Gamarnikow, 1978), who carry
out the nursing role, are apparently tied into a socially con-
structed picture of formally carrying out women's work.
This in turn has had the effect of legitimizing the lower status given to nurse caring, particularly in relation to the care
given by those in the medical and allied scientific professions (see Game and Pringle, 1983; Oakley, 1984).

Salvage (1990) acknowledges the many efforts made by
nurses to challenge these prevailing images, which serve to
downgrade nurse care by implying that it is natural and
intuitive women's work, rather than an occupation, pre-
dominantly composed of women, who are involved with
giving care of a professional nature. She would like to see a
much greater emphasis placed by nurses on the analysis,
understanding, and response to the wider and fundamental

societal issues about power and gender. For in the end, society's attitude to women and women's work is central to the vision and worth it ascribes to nurses and nursing, and as such to its professional credibility.

Sadly, nursing as an occupational group has spent more time historically contemplating itself and its internal strategies within the health service. This without a doubt has promoted important theoretical developments, improved understanding, and advanced practice in line with new health care needs. However, according to Witts (1992), modern definitions of what nursing is all about are 'both numerous and diverse' and continue to 'reflect the relationship of nursing as a jack-of-all trades support system to medicine and its allied occupations.' It would appear then that in spite of internal effort by nurses to grow and develop as professionals alongside medicine, it has largely failed. It does appear that persistent attention to internal strategies alone are unlikely to alter the root causes of nurse professional subordination to the medical profession.

Etzioni's (1969) semi-professional notion then may well be a fair reflection of the less secure professional base on which nursing stands. Nonetheless, even as a semi-profession, nurses are seen as knowledgeable and are well respected by the general public. Sadly, however, it is suggested that this is only as a result of their long term working relationship with doctors. As Bridges (1991) said 'One reason for the continued use of the medical model for nursing is the high value placed by society on biological survival resulting in a high status for those disciplines associated with medicine.' Again, this adherence to the medical profession and the metaphorical 'rubbing of shoulders', whilst providing a halo effect, does not address the disparity in status between doctors and nurses, and how the balance might be changed. It merely reinforces the dependent position of nursing to medicine, and does not encourage a truly collegiate relationship between the groups, which offer complementary, but different, caring roles in society. So it would appear then, that efforts over time to become a full profession have not succeeded. Attempts to professionalize the role by developing in-depth knowledge, expertise and specialization, and by the shedding of non-nursing work (for example sterilization of instruments, preparation of dressings, domestic work and clerical duties), all have apparently been to little avail. By comparison, similar moves to specialization by doctors have met with much more effective outcomes for them (Heller, 1978).

It is clear then that if nursing is ever to take on the coveted title of a full profession, it will need to give greater attention to two important aspects. Firstly, it should develop its understanding and activity around those external political forces which shape society's attitudes to women and women in work. Secondly, nursing will at the same time need to establish its own mission in terms of caring, and to explain it more clearly than hitherto. In this way, status could be given to its caring role rather than to that of assistant to medical practice. Admittedly, this is not likely to be an easy task, judging by what we have seen so far in this chapter. There are those who doubt the need to employ qualified nurses at present levels, and others who view nurses as 'bit players' who should turn their hand to any task or speciality if staffing levels dictate. The support for, and promotion of care assistants and support workers to carry out caring tasks, has also served to rebut claims as to the professional nature of nursing care.

It therefore becomes increasingly evident that nurses need to understand what is happening to them in the present day NHS, so that they can respond to what appears to be a gradual management-inspired dismantling of professional nurse development. As we will see, the nursing profession, however defined, is apparently under challenge within the newly reformed NHS. Indeed, we need to remind ourselves that Government health policy has been working towards this situation for over a decade. So let us reflect back first on what has taken place in the NHS and on how we find ourselves today under such a threat.

Professionalism under attack

As already noted, both doctors and nurses have developed their professional roles to a greater or lesser degree. The obvious centrality of their contribution to the workings of a health service have ensured over time both autonomy and great power in the decision-making process. Certainly, in the early 1980s, the professionals had greater power than the managers and administrators. However, the federation inevitable in an organization as dependent upon professionals as the NHS, meant that there was no single focal point of power or decision making. It was because of this lack of clarity in the management process that the Government determined to introduce a series of changes designed to strengthen NHS management. No group in the health service whether professional or manual was to be left untouched, least of all nurses, in what was to be a systematic overhaul of the whole service. Whereas previous governments and their health ministers failed to pursue and hold on to the professional reins, the Conservative governments since 1979 have pulled themselves firmly into the driving seat and attempted to make the health care agendas of all professionals and non-professionals alike fall into line.

General management

For some the introduction of general management in early 1980s was regarded as an attack both on professional autonomy and clinical freedoms. It thus attracted a predictably hostile reception from both doctors and nurses. However, Griffiths and his inquiry team (Griffiths, 1983) must have expected nothing less. Their specific remit had been to make an assessment of NHS management. It came as no surprise that they concluded that the clear power of professional groups overrode management decision making. The inquiry team had found that the multiplicity of professional role players in the NHS, all demanding that their voice be heard in management circles, led to consensus decisions which were not sharp enough to manage effectively, and also ensured that NHS change was slow and incremental. General management, as in industrial settings was proposed as a more successful route to take. As in business circles, a knowledge of levels and quality of service, of costs, of employee motivation, of evaluation of services and a commitment to the 'real' consumer of the NHS was needed. All of these proposed changes were presented as the only way of moving forward, to ensure value for money for the taxpayer, together with the provision of an effective and efficient health service which benefitted the whole community.

The new management

In the wake of the Griffiths report, all RHAs, DHAs and NHS hospitals (in England) were ordered to appoint general managers by the end of 1985. Together new managers throughout the NHS were to assume responsibility for overall direction and strategic management of the British health care service. A line management funding developed on clear business principles was thereby introduced to the NHS. General managers were mainly in position by 1986 (Holliday, 1992), with only 36 of these new-style managers being nurses (Brindle, 1993d).

The managers, in the main, plucked from industrial backgrounds, were brought into the NHS to make the necessary changes. Short-term contracts, performance related pay and reviews were introduced to help sharpen their commitment and resolve to deliver the required managerial policies throughout the NHS. Whilst manual workers had already felt the sharp edge of compulsory competitive tendering since 1984, nurses and doctors were now set to feel the impact of a new managerial philosophy which required everyone to come under sharp commercial scrutiny and prove their worth if they were to stay in business in the NHS.

The nurses – what happened to them?

Nursing hierarchies were dismantled, including the demise of the traditional matron figures. This in particular represented a rejection of previous professional values with nurses gaining reward for time served in the NHS. In its place came new ideas linking reward and career opportunities to skills, experience and managerial ability. Disappointment was expressed at the low numbers of nurses who became general managers, but then judging from the Griffiths' Report, little credence was given to nurses as potential general management material anyway. Added to all of this, the regrading developments concerning nurse pay in 1987 caused a furore inspiring thousands to take industrial action (Pilkington, 1989). In addition to providing an environment of divide and rule between nurses, it opened up wounds which still exist today. Many regarding appeals are still outstanding, and some hospital and community units have tried to buy out those involved with golden handshakes, (Editorial, Nursing Times 1993a). The divisions look set to continue.

The doctors

Doctors also felt extremely challenged by the new managerial culture slipping into the NHS in the mid 1980s. However, appeals to their sense of responsibility in serving the public well, particularly in a period of economic stringency, provided the backcloth to other managerial strategies. Doctors were encouraged to become responsible for clinical budgeting, and to be involved in the use of performance reviews and indicators. All of these enabled management to make comparisons on activity between clinicians. In addition to this, and too oil the wheels of change, improved distinction awards were offered to consultants. Some doctors became general managers, but others were not convinced at that stage by the changes, and others still hold out today. In the years following, many doctors and nurses continued to try to work as they had done before the introduction of general management, conceding small points to survive. It was obvious to the Government that further reform was needed to develop the required cultural change, and to force the professions into a context in which they had to become a working part of the new businesslike NHS or to leave.

The old ways of running a service in which professionals maintained secrecy and thus power in their work, was poised to be overthrown even further by the internal market reforms of April 1991. The managed competition between the purchasers and providers of the services would both open up and sharpen the delivery of professional practice. Those who delivered 'the business' would benefit financially, as would their employer institution, those who did not would lose out.

As Mangan says: 'Nurses need to demonstrate their worth if they want to remain clinicians, teachers, and managers in the new NHS' (Mangan, 1993). We will consider this next as we reflect on our experience so far, and try to decide if the nursing profession is indeed under threat from the NHS reforms.

The NHS reforms – further challenges to nurses?

By January 1989 the move to general management, according to the Secretary of State for Health in the White Paper *Working for Patients* (Department of Health, 1989) was showing results and pointing the way ahead. New management information systems had shown variations in performance up and down the country, different waiting times for care depending on where one lived, and variations in drug prescribing habits and referral rates. For the Secretary of State, professionals of all descriptions could do much better in putting the patients first.

The ways to achieve this laudable objective were set out in the White Paper which Kenneth Clarke, Secretary of State for Health, presented to the House of Commons in a health service debate on 31 January 1989. The details in the Hansard Report are both illuminating and interesting for all nurses (Hansard, 1989). A brief look at just some of the points made will be of use to the discussion.

The White Paper debate – the politicians' view (Hansard, 1989)

The announcement of the reforms prompted sharp responses from the opposition benches. Robin Cook, Labour Party Shadow Health Secretary, clearly aware of the managerial activity we have discussed, wondered:

How many more bureaucrats the NHS will need to make this package work? Will he tell us how much time doctors will have to take off patient care to file their financial returns? Will he tell us how much more the monitoring, the pricing and the bargaining over every treatment will add to the cost of administration, and whether a single closed ward will reopen as a result of this White Paper?

Cook also queried the lack of discussion with the caring professions involved in the health service. In response Clarke said:

There is no reason why the public service should not be run with the same efficiency and consumer consciousness as the private sector – he [Cook] cannot dismiss the value of modern management disciplines, financial accountability and consumer consciousness that we are seeking to build into the health service.

As far as the lack of consultation with nurses and doctors was concerned, Clarke said that he would talk with them after the publication of a variety of working papers which would provide greater detail of specific changes to be introduced.

As the debate moved on, one back-bench Labour MP Michael Foot again raised the interests of professionals:

Will the Right Hon. and learned gentleman now tell us whether he is proposing to have any genuine consultations with people working in the service: with the nurses, the unions, the British Medical Association, and the presidents of the royal colleges?

Clarke's repudiation of speaking to representative groups only, rather than to all staff was clear in his response. He stated:

The Labour Party's idea of consultation on health policy, as we all know, is to ring up NUPE, reversing the charges, and ask what they should be expected to say. We propose to run the Health Service in an altogether more constructive fashion.

It would appear then that nurse representative organizations were to be circumvented, and importantly even the largest did not merit mention by name, as they were all lumped together dismissively under NUPE, for fairly obvious reasons. As Audrey Wise, Labour back-bench MP, suggested, the reason why the professions had not been involved in the review in the first place, was that they might have got in the way of the imposition of the changes because they would have disagreed with the whole process. Indeed, Clarke was accused by Dr Lewis Moonie (Labour MP) of only having a tenuous grasp on reality:

> The proposal is born of the eccentric mind of someone in the Adam Smith institute who has no concept of what it is like to run a health service, as opposed to talking and thinking about one.

All in all the parliamentary debate confirmed the feeling that the managerial and market reforms were to be driven through with or without the professionals. None of this, of course, sounded particularly propitious for the development of the nursing profession. Perhaps we need to look for hints within the White Paper itself so that we can piece together the jigsaw and try to find some answers to our questions around potential nurse professionalism in the post-reform future.

Clues from the White Paper (Department of Health, 1989)

Promises to the nurses from the White Paper included greater satisfaction and rewards for those working in the NHS who successfully respond to local needs and preferences. The Trusts, it said, would harness the skills and dedication of the staff, and would be setting their own conditions, pay rates and rewards for individual performances. A better use of professional staff and their skills was also promised, together with the provision of better training for non-professional support staff. An appraisal of the traditional practices of nurses would result in some doctor tasks being passed to them, and some clerical work taken away. Linked to all of the above was the promise that the nursing profession would become part of resource management initiatives to provide management with more information about nurse care activity and its cost.

Even the initial announcement of the proposed changes and the introduction of market reforms suggested a conflict with the growing professional aspirations of nurses. These concerns have sadly started to be borne out by experience. For example, the pressure to contain costs of NHS spending, the persistent development of the managerial culture and commercialization, the search for cost-effective clinical effectiveness, a reassessment of skill–mix and possible labour substitutions, and a determined effort to raise the calibre of untrained staff to take on nursing roles, all clearly contribute to a questioning of the supposed special nature of professional nurse expertise and status.

As was said earlier, professionals perceive they have autonomy in their practice, and by virtue of their superior skills and knowledge know more than other people what is required to give good, holistic patient care. Backed up by the UKCC Code of Conduct which underpins nurse practice, nurses offer a 'guarantee of integrity' (Kaye in Prandy, 1965), both to those who employ them, and to those who receive their care. However, if management now seek to both shape, control and reduce nurse practice, then they may be clearly denigrating efforts made in very recent times to professionalize nursing both through practice developments and educational change.

New nurse agendas for professionalism

According to Thomas (1993) 'nursing is standing up well to a government that is not committed to professionalisation.' He notes that 'the impact of management-led organisations, significant education reform, demographic decline and difficulties in recruiting staff' have all impacted upon a profession which feels under siege now that the reforms are well under way. However, nurses have not just been reactive recipients of these and earlier changes. They have sought to strengthen, develop and change nursing's professional rationale as society also has changed in its structure and created new health needs to be met. The 'New Nursing' approaches have been taken on (Salvage, 1988). According to Beardshaw and Robinson (1990) the changes implicit with this involved 'moves to replace the task-based method of organising nursing work, with care more precisely tailored to individual patient needs.' In doing so, it sought, 'to substitute a professional model of organisation for nursing's long-established hierarchical bureaucratic one.'

These developments, according to Salvage provided the ideological underpinning for both the reform of nurse education in Project 2000 (UKCC, 1986), and for clinical career restructuring (Salvage, 1990).

Gaze (1991) also looked to professionalizing changes which have met with some success: the emergence of primary nursing, nurse practitioners and nurse consultants. However, it is clear that any future developments will depend upon how much support nurses are given by government and thus by health service management. This is an interesting scenario to consider, for according to Elkan and Robinson (1993):

> The goals of the reformers and those of the government have not been wholly incompatible . . . the aim of distinguishing between basic care workers and an élite group of

professional nurses has been favourably looked up by government, since this is consistent with the managerial goal of rationalising health care by giving higher rewards and status to skilled professional workers while reducing the cost of providing unskilled basic care.

So, the professional reformers could ironically find themselves sharing an agenda with management. With the pressure to reduce nurse labour costs, and with the desire to introduce localized pay bargaining into the NHS Trusts, there may well be an implicit bargain whereby a few nurses achieve higher salaries and greater professional status, whilst others, who may even currently be called nurses, will be downgraded in pay, security and status. This two-tier structure of employment amongst nurses would paradoxically for the first time in the history of the NHS give the fortunate few real bargaining power with their employer.

The question for nurses and their organizations is whether they want to close their doors, tighten their profession, become an élite, and in so doing differentiate themselves from others who may also be performing caring roles in the NHS.

Potential for other practice developments?

It is worth saying that any other new developments in nursing will also, judging from experience, face many challenges. Anything which seeks to change established practice is fraught with obstacles, even from within the profession itself. Moves to take up ground held by the medical profession is likely to be met with some ferocity. Also, any uncosted or unproved activity, however promising in theory, is open to question compared with well-tried and well understood former practices. Qualified nursing care is a costly resource in the NHS budgeting equation. Because of this, no matter how nursing reprepares and redefines its roles, nurses like any other part of the labour market are under very close scrutiny and subject to vigorous questioning as to their professed special status.

According to Eric Caines at a manager's conference, 'nurses only spend 5% of their time on exercising their skills: the rest goes on random care . . . Random care was the job of support workers and nurses should do a clinical job purely and simply.' The NHS reforms provided a good opportunity to 'reshape the nursing profession', although he recognized 'there would be a lot of resistance and many nurses would feel hurt and upset by what people do to them' (in Hart, 1991).

Have the reforms then proved really uncomfortable for nurses, and have they been able to make much progress in their efforts to professionalize?

The Reforms: whistleblowing: a professional step too far?

The need to meet service requirements in the most cost-effective way has certainly provided a difficult backcloth to potential nurse professional developments. Issues concerning autonomy of practice, pay commensurate with skills and knowledge and with comparable occupations, credibility of the nurse role and support for new developments in caring are all under threat. The nursing press has been full of worrying individual and group experiences of the reforms, amongst many other things, relating to standards of care and to professional developments. A brief look at the whistleblowing issues will help to highlight some of the problems felt by nurses.

Only a month after the implementation of the reforms in

April 1991, press reports described NHS management as beginning a process of restricting NHS staff from speaking out against the changes (Editorial, *Guardian*, 1991). Calls to restore the medical and nursing professionals' right to free speech without confidentiality clauses in contracts were widely discussed and reported.

According to Waterhouse (1991):

> Doctors, nurses and hospital staff who speak out against the Government's NHS reforms – in particular its plans for hospitals to become self-governing trusts – are being threatened with dismissal. Since the NHS reforms came into effect on 1st April, some authorities have imposed new 'confidentiality' policies without debate, in what the Royal College of Nursing describes as a 'climate of intimidation'.

Almost inevitably examples have occurred of cases of individuals who in expressing their concerns about aspects of NHS standards or practice have found themselves subject to disciplinary procedures.

- Graham Pink described his concerns about the lack of staff on wards for elderly people in Stepping Hill Hospital, Stockport (Bolger, 1990; Brindle, 1990).
- Dr Helen Zeitlin spoke out against nursing shortages at Alexandra Hospital, Redditch, and was dismissed on grounds of redundancy (Snell, 1992).
- Dr Chris Chapman (Biochemist, Leeds General Infirmary Trust) was sacked after he had unearthed a scientific fraud and gone public. He was given notice after the reorganization of the pathology department at LGI and was the only member of the 200 strong department to lose his job (Hugill, 1992).

Not so well reported or known about was the threat by St Bartholomew's College of Nursing to discipline 22 third year students who had complained about standards of care in two clinical placements (Nursing Times, 1992). The threat was removed after they had apologized for the offence they had caused by their letter. Incidentally, their complaints were acted upon, which suggests they were probably right in the first place. One could argue that this particular experience may well have ensured that some of them will keep their thoughts to themselves in the future – hardly helpful in encouraging them to apply their code of conduct (their badge of professional 'integrity') in future times, when another bad care experience faces them.

Rundell however suggests that some nurses would actually prefer a full-blown gagging clause in their contract because this would avoid the obvious unpleasantness surrounding speaking out (Rundell, 1992). As Wright explained:

> The history of nursing is littered with the names of those lost to the profession who were unable to pursue and sustain a complaint. People like Mr Pink who hit the headlines are in the minority; thousands more are unable or unwilling to follow this path (Wright, 1990).

Indeed, according to an MSF (Manufacturing, Science and Finance Union) survey:

> Nurses are less likely to 'whistleblow' about standards of care than any other group of NHS employees – nurses were the most 'vulnerable' and were afraid to speak out because they had neither the independent status of GPs nor the seniority of consultants (MSF, 1993).

This is a sad conclusion because nurses clearly do have concerns about the NHS. An RCN survey for example, (Brindle, 1993a) which questioned 2000 nurses found:

- almost two in three nurses believed that there are too few staff on their ward to provide proper patient care; and

● only one in five is confident that managers would act on concerns about staffing.

In a sense here we see the dilemma for nurses. They clearly know the issues which should be raised, but they are either frightened or they feel that there is little use in speaking out. Indeed, if they know anything about those who have hit the headlines and lost their jobs in the process, it is little wonder they do keep quiet. As Derek Fatchett MP said at the launch of the pressure group 'Freedom to Care': 'Nurses and doctors who tell the truth about care in the NHS risk the sack' (Fatchett, 1992).

Can we believe Duncan Nichol's words on launching the new government guidelines on whistleblowing? (NHS Management Executive, 1993b). He said that 'it was important to encourage openness and dialogue in the NHS where the free expression by staff of their concerns are welcomed by their managers as a contribution towards improving services' (Snell, 1993b). Responses to the document have included it being described as a 'gagger's charter' and 'creating a climate of fear', and a 'press gag on health staff' (Brindle, 1993b).

Many of the commentators again refer to the dissonance between the Government's expressed wishes, and the action taken on their behalf in the NHS. Nichol asserts that the NHS exists to meet the needs of patients, and affirms the duty of all employees to draw to the attention of their managers any matter they consider to be damaging the interests of patients and clients. That is all very well, but according to one editor:

> The guidance does not deal with the possible disputes over large policy issues such as funding and staffing levels. There is no room here for the nurse who speaks out because he or she feels the quality of patient care is being adversely affected by government policy (Editorial, *Nursing Times*, 1993b).

If this is the case, then so much for the Nurse Code of Conduct. It would seem that in this particular respect any claim to professional autonomy in practice is open to question. Whilst there are those who remind us that there always has been in the 'lineage of nursing a tradition of compliance' (Rowden, 1992), we need to view the moves in recent years to quieten any potential dissenting voice as something quite different in character.

Widening the professional credibility gap?

Along with gagging clauses in contracts, and government guidelines on how to complain, professional autonomy is seen by many as clearly under threat. At the same time, nurses have fallen behind in terms of pay with comparable occupations such as the police and the fire brigade (Cole, 1993; Laurent, 1993). According to Christine Hancock the 1993 pay award had dealt yet another blow to the nursing profession which would have serious long-term effects. It would ensure that nursing continued to be seen by others as a 'low-paid, undervalued profession' (Friend, 1993).

Also, coupled with all the outstanding regrading appeals (Hempel, 1993), performance related pay is looming on the horizon and an ever deepening implementation of skill mixing. It is also worth remembering the earlier note impact of the reforms (i.e. the apparent rise in manager appointments, as against the well reported drop in the employment of qualified nurses) (Brindle, 1993c; Editorial, *Nursing Times*, 1993c).

According to Malcolm Wing, representing UNISON, the agenda behind the plummeting figures, he believed, was a move towards a casualization of the workforce. He said that bank staff numbers were rising and now accounted for 6.7% of the nursing workforce. He pointed out that employers were using bank staff when they needed them and were not offering nurses job security (Wing, 1993).

Nursing's professionalizing strategy seems to be descending into a shambles. Nurses appear to be more controlled in what they say, and how they work. Derisory pay awards tend to suggest that the government feel that they have the upper hand over the largest workforce in health care and can pay salaries which suggest anything but professional credibility. Nursing as a group is expected to deliver the government's vision for health care (NHS Management Executive, 1993a) but in return the credibility being sought as true professionals is surely not forthcoming.

Summary

This discussion has considered a variety of issues about the nature of professionalism with particular emphasis on nursing. The backcloth to the debate has been the NHS reforms, which we know from previous chapters appears to be producing some worrying outcomes. Our conclusion at this point must still be one of concern and fears for the future of nursing as a profession.

On the one hand the managerial trends which have been encouraged since the early 1980s are slowly but surely tightening the grip on nurse activity. On the other hand, there are those who appear to be in favour of dismantling the nursing profession, and are looking forward to the creation of a two-tier system of health carers. One tier will be made up of an élite minority of well-paid nurse professionals who will manage and organize care, and the other, lesser tier will be made up of non-professional carers who will carry out the prescribed tasks needed to keep the NHS in business.

As was said at the beginning of this chapter: 'The golden age of certainty about long-term careers in, and general support for nursing as a developing profession is under threat.' The NHS reforms have clearly thrown the future of nursing as a profession into the air. Who knows where it will land, and who will benefit the most?

References

Beardshaw Virginia and Robinson Ray (1990) *New for Old? Prospects For Nursing In The 1990's*. No. 8. Research Report Series Current Health Policy Issues. Kings Fund Institute.

Becker HS (1970) *Sociological Work*. London, Allen Lane.

Bolger Tom (1990) Can you hear the whistle? *Nursing Times* **86**(18).

Bridges Jacqueline (1991) Distinct from medicine. *Nursing Times*, **87**(27).

Brindle David (1990) Yours sincerely, F.G. Pink. *The Guardian*, April 11.

Brindle David (1993a) Nurses say too few staff for proper patient care. *The Guardian*, May 17.

Brindle David (1993b) Press 'gag' on health staff. *The Guardian*, June 10.

Brindle David (1993c) NHS private patient income soars. *The Guardian*, July 30.

Brindle David (1993d) Doctors, nurses . . . and managers. *The Guardian*, September 29 (Health Appointments p 15).

Caines Eric (1993) Amputation is crucial to the patient's health. *The Guardian*, May 11.

Cohen Phil (1993) United fronts? *Nursing Times*, **89**(26).

Cole Andrew (1993) Body blow. *Nursing Times*, **89**(8).

Department of Health (1989) *Working For Patients*. Cmd. 555. London, HMSO.

Downey Rachel (1993). Call for freeze on student intakes. *Nursing Times*, **89**(14).

Durkheim E (1951) *Suicide: A Study in Sociology*, Free Press.

Editorial (Guardian) (1991) Stealthy is not very healthy. *The Guardian*, May 20.

Editorial (Nursing Times) (1993a) The shambles goes on. *Nursing Times*, **89**(7).

Editorial (Nursing Times) (1993b) A charter with no teeth. *Nursing Times*, **89**(24).

Editorial (Nursing Times) (1993c) Alarming drop in qualified staff numbers. *Nursing Times*, **89**(3).

Elkan R and Robinson J (1993) Project 2000. Back to basics. *Nursing Times*, **89**(4).

Etzioni Amitai (1969) *The Semi-Professions And Their Organisation: Teachers, Nurses, Social Workers*. New York, Free Press.

Fatchett Derek MP (1992) Government guidance on free speech given cool response. *Nursing Times*, **88**(47).

Faugier Jean (1992) Tall poppies. *Nursing Times*, **88**(50).

Friedson E (1970) *The Profession of Medicine*. New York, Dodd Mead.

Friend Bernadette (1993) Unions Protest at derisory 1.5% rise. *Nursing Times*, **89**(7).

Game A, and Pringle R (1983) *Gender at Work*. London, Pluto Press.

Gamarnikow E (1978) Sexual division of labour: the case in nursing, in Kuhn A and Wolpe A (eds) *Feminism and Materialism*. London, Routledge and Kegan Paul.

Gaze Harriett (1991) Changing images. *Nursing Times*, **87**(20).

Greenwood E (1957) Attributes of a profession. *Social Work* **2**(3) 44–45.

Griffiths Roy (1983) *NHS Management Inquiry*. London, Department of Health.

Hancock Christine (1993) Cutbacks Offer Grim Prospect For Patients, (Letter) *The Guardian*, May 12th.

Hart Elizabeth (1991) Ghost in the machine. *Health Service Journal*, December 5.

Hansard (Parliamentary Debates) (1989) Statement. *NHS Review*. **146**(39).

Heller Tom (1978) *Restructuring The Health Service*. London, Croom Helm.

Hempel Sandra (1993) Buying-out appeals. *Nursing Times*, **89**(5).

Holliday Ian (1992) *The NHS Transformed*. Manchester, Baseline Books.

Hugman R (1991) *Power in Caring Professions*. Houndmills, Macmillan.

Hugill Barry (1992) Fraud probe after hospital sacks its whistle-blower. *The Observer*, October 11.

Johnson Terence J (1972) *Professions and Power*. London, Macmillan.

Kaye B in Prandy Kenneth (1965) *Professional Employees*. London, Faber and Faber.

Laurent Claire (1993) Professional position. *Nursing Times*, **89**(8).

Mangan Paul (1993) Survival of the fittest. *Nursing Times*, **89**(6).

McEvoy Patrick (1992) The professionals. *Nursing Times*, **88**(9).

Millerson Geoffrey (1964) *The Qualifying Associations: A Study In Professionalism*. London, Routledge and Kegan Paul.

MSF (Manufacturing, Science and Finance Union) (1993) Nursing staff too afraid to speak out on standards of care. *Nursing Times*, **89**(9).

Murray Tom (1990) The college's response to the ambulance dispute does not reflect credit on nursing. *Nursing Times*, **86**(7).

NHS Management Executive (1993) *A Vision For The Future*. London, Department of Health.

NHS Management Executive (1993) *Guidance For Staff On Relations With The Public And The Media*. London, Department of Health.

Nightingale Florence (1881) *Letter to Probationer Nurses at St. Thomas's Hospital* (In Nightingale Collection LSE).

Nursing Times (1992) *College Drops Action As Students Apologise*. **88**(41).

Oakley A (1984) What price professionalism? The importance of being a nurse. *Nursing Times*, **7**.

Parsons T (1939) The professions and the social structure *Social Forces*, **17**, 457–67.

Parsons T (1951) *The Social System*. London, Routledge and Kegan Paul.

Peters BG et al. (1978) In Lewis PG, Potter DC and Castles FG (eds). *The Practice of Comparative Politics*. Longman.

Pilkington Edward (1989) Angels with battered wings. *The Guardian*, November 29.

Robinson J in Snell Janet (1993) Far fewer nurses needed, says Caines. *Nursing Times*, **89**(20).

Robinson J (1991) Power, politics and policy analysis in nursing, in Perry A and Jolley M (eds) *Nursing: a Knowledge Base for Practice*. London, Edward Arnold.

Robinson K in Robinson J, Gray A and Elkan R (eds) (1992) *Policy Issues in Nursing*, Milton Keynes, Open University Press.

Rowden Ray (1992) Self-imposed silence. *Nursing Times*, **88**(24).

Rundell Simon (1991) Who wants to be a doctor? *Nursing Times*, **87**(1).

Rundell Simon (1992) Bound up. *Nursing Times*, **88**(37).

Salvage Jane (1988) Professionalisation – or struggle for survival? *Journal of Advanced Nursing* **13**, 515–519.

Salvage Jane (1990) The theory and practice of the new nursing. *Nursing Times*, **86**(4). 42–5.

Shelley Howard (1990) Why tall poppies are not popular. *Nursing Times*, **89**(4).

Snell Janet (1992) Whistle-blowing doctor to get job back. *Nursing Times*, **88**(46).

Snell Janet (1993a) Far fewer nurses needed, says Caines. *Nursing Times*, **89**(20).

Snell Janet (1993b) Whistleblower guide comes under attack. *Nursing Times*, **89**(24).

Thomas Ben (1993) A dilution of skills. *Nursing Times*, **89**(29).

Turner Bryan S (1991) *Medical Power and Social Knowledge*. London, Sage Publications.

United Kingdom Central Council (1986) *Project 2000: A New Preparation for Practice*. London, UKCC.

Waterhouse Rosie (1991) NHS staff gagged on health reforms. *Independent on Sunday*, May 12.

Watkins Stephen J. The trouble with nursing. *Health Visitor*, **65**(10).

Weber M (1966) *The Sociology of Religion*. London, Methuen.

Wing Malcolm (1993) Alarming drop in qualified staff numbers. *Nursing Times*, **89**(30).

Witts Paul (1992) in Soothill K, Henry C and Kendrick K (eds) *Themes and Perspectives in Nursing*. London, Chapman and Hall.

Wright Stephen (1990) How the nurses can gain the power to speak out. *The Guardian*, August 25.

6

Drawing the Strands Together

The discussions in this book have been about developing a concern for two important aspects:

- The survival of a national health service.
- The future development of the nursing profession.

Whilst well known earlier writers took up the initial task of encouraging nurses to be political, and to shape their own professional destiny, in this case the work builds upon their precedent. The analysis of some aspects of the NHS reforms will hopefully act as a catalyst for an informed and practical response to what is happening to both the NHS and to nurses in the 1990s.

The scene has been set mainly in the early experience of what appears to be the most profound set of changes endured within the National Health Service since its inception in 1948. It has been argued that these changes reflect a rebuilding of the NHS into a market model of health care distribution. Within it we have seen the appearance of purchasers and providers, and also the rapid development of a new underpinning ethos which is both commercialized and competitive in nature.

At the same time, and as a by-product of such a major systematic overhaul, we are seeing what appears to be a redefinition of nursing practice into yet another manageable and marketable commodity to be sold and bought in this business of health care. The root and branch reform of the NHS is clearly leaving no part untouched or unchanged, be it structure or personnel. Nurses therefore have a clear interest in understanding what is happening to them today, if they aspire to any future role enrichment or opportunity for full-blown professional status.

The discussions have as a consequence revolved around four aspects of the NHS changes which are central to nurse practice:

- The internal health care market – the environment of nursing care;
- The consumers – those who receive nurse care;
- Health promotion – the focus or limitations of nurse care; and
- Nurses in the NHS – the professional dimension of care.

All the debates have highlighted different but linking impacts of the reforms, on both the NHS context within which most nurses work, and because of the knock-on effects, on the content of the care provided by them. In turn this has serious implications for the professional dimension of nursing, and any future development.

If the tentative conclusions of this book are correct, and the changes in the NHS are in contradistinction to the professional values of nurses, what, then, should be the response?

A professional code of conduct would infer that the primary duty of the professional nurse was to his or her patient, and not to the management of the service. So at this point, there is potential conflict, a dilemma for nurses: to speak out or not, when it is claimed, contrary to our own experience, that all is well.

Suffice to say at this stage, the daily news reports on the NHS continue to develop many of the concerns and themes already expressed in the earlier chapters. Whilst some of these might have raised accusations of shroud-waving, perhaps by now, what might have initially been perceived as rhetoric, may sadly have become a reality in practice for many readers. According to one commentator:

> The pillars of the Government's health policy are crumbling, rank weeds protrude from its cracking facade to reveal not sound foundations but merely a clever *trompe-l'œil*. Almost three years into John Major's premiership, the politics of illusion rule at the Department of Health: symbol triumphs over substance, rhetoric over reality (Davies, 1993).

All nurses will know of anectodal evidence of things going wrong in the health service of today. Indeed, judging from the recent nursing press, few will be unaware of the very real feelings of demoralization of many within the nursing profession. So what has happened to create this feeling? What can be done to turn it around? Firstly, let us remind ourselves of some of the issues raised in the previous chapters.

In Chapter 2 the imposition of the internal health care market was found to have had some well-reported serious teething problems. At the same time, arguments were made to the contrary by those who saw a success story replacing the failure of previous times. They remind us of the inefficiencies, the long waiting lists, the inability to listen to the users of the services, the lack of knowledge about costs, quality or outcomes. The new model NHS was in every way perceived as an improvement, and its further development supported, even for some as far as a privatized medical service with limited intervention from the state.

However, consistent with Chapter 2, it appears that the negative stories are continuing to appear with monotonous regularity. The NHS has been likened to the crumbling cliffs of Scarborough, with bits of the service becoming day by day unavailable to patients. Staff involved have become confused and demoralized by the market changes which have been variously described as 'a maelstrom out of control' (Ross, 1993), and 'a monster which is uncontrollable in its actions and effects' (Mason, 1993).

The need to fit financial cash flows, rather than to meet need, has according to some, clearly distorted care provision. Some hospitals have had to stop operating theatre work well before the end of the financial year because annual surgical budgets have been used up too quickly. Sadly, patients still on their waiting lists have been waiting on average 18 months for admission for surgery (Editorial, *Sunday Observer*, 1993). Other widespread reports concern the creation of a two-tier NHS service, with for example, preference being given to fund-holding general practitioners who have been able to get fast-track care for their clients, as opposed to those practices who are not budget holders. Related to this has been the suggestion that this has resulted in people from the most deprived areas receiving a second rate service (Ross, 1993). Similarly, others have expressed concern as to the lack of regulatory mechanisms within the internal health care market to protect the special interests of ethnic minorities and other vulnerable users of the health service as it is now organized (Karmi, 1993).

The Shadow Health Secretary, David Blunkett, has accused the Government of presiding over market-style health service changes which he describes as an expensive failure (Blunkett, 1993). He has also responded angrily to the appearance of new advertisements by private health insurers, which suggest by implication in their adverts that the NHS is being privatized because it cannot cope (Brindle 1993b). His appeals to the Health Secretary to ban them may well fall on stony ground. After all, the increasingly close relationship being encouraged by the Government between the NHS and the private sector does give reasonable cause for concern – suggestion at this stage, perhaps becoming father to the deed in the future?

Alongside all these structural and organizational faults, is the creation of a culture of closed administration which forbids open criticism of it, and by implication, if not intention, appears to remove the ethos of care and responsibility. Any open challenge to the new system is seen as disloyal, destructive, and a challenge to the corporate image. No nurse should be unaware of the fate of whistleblowers.

This apparent closing down or heading off of challenges not only applies to those within the NHS, but also to the general public who have been undemocratically removed from representation on NHS bodies and denied access to information. The NHS Management Executive has even had to create its own 'good news' department to remind everyone, public and professional alike, of the great successes achieved (Brindle, 1993a). Of course, the present Health Secretary herself persistently reminds us of the achievements of the internal health care market, noting that patients have seen steady improvements in both the quantity and quality of the services. Perhaps a final overall thought following our brief look at Chapter 2 might be that nurses should be forgiven if they do not feel quite the same amount of conviction as Mrs Bottomley, when they reflect on their own experiences so far in the new NHS market.

Moving on to Chapter 3 we looked at the consumers in the NHS, and found that in spite of avowals to the contrary, they were apparently not being further empowered by the changes. Instead, they appear as mere pawns in some more important political game being played by Government as it develops and shapes its new market-led health service.

Within the internal health care market they are not the true purchasers of care, but are 'represented' by the GPs and the health authorities who buy services on their behalf. In addition, the already mentioned fact that public representatives have been removed from planning and decision-making bodies, challenges the truth of any claim to the development of a new and true consumerist approach. The well-reported patient charters have also faced accusations of being mere frills and window dressing. They appear to lack any real financial backing or any serious intention of power for consumers. Indeed, judging from the earlier reports of two-tiering, cancellations of operations, budgets running out, and services being taken out of NHS remits, it seems that consumers, and very specifically the most vulnerable, may well be getting a rawer deal that previously. Whilst we know that nurses have tried to be more responsive to consumer needs, they alone cannot counter the negative effects of the distribution system of the internal market which is based on competition, and thus implies winners and losers. Whilst the previous NHS model, with all its short-falls, aspired to some sort of equitable distribution of health care for all of the population, surely the ethos of the present model is not based on the same foundations. We should all, as nurses, feel seriously concerned at this conclusion, particularly when we acknowledge the equal importance of all clients or users of the health service, but know that the reality in practice may well be very different.

In Chapter 4 doubts were expressed as to the Government's intention for the NHS to head and control the much lauded *Health of the Nation* strategy. Whilst acknowledging that it appears to give endorsement for a health promotion mission for the NHS, a closer examination of intentions for action suggests something very different.

It has been said by many that the document is an expression of government hypocrisy. It makes little or no effort to consider the root causes of much ill-health such as poverty, inequality, unemployment and low economic status. Instead it emphasizes the need for individual behaviour change to reduce the trends in specific pathological outcomes, and gives no credence to, or acknowledgement of, the additional need for new macro-economic policies to mitigate some of the well-reported ill effects of the present-day recession. According to one UNISON member at a recent conference of the Trades Union Congress, Government policies are contributing directly to a drastic decline in public health. She condemned the complacency of the Government as it prescribed over the re-emergence and revival of the old diseases of poverty such as tuberculosis (Harrison, 1993).

The document setting out the health strategy offered no extra legislation or binding roles for other ministerial departments, no extra cash to support new activity, and only urges collaborative action via healthy alliances with other state institutions and independent organizations. This last point might sound good, but in reality is a difficult act to deliver. We need to remember that the other statutory bodies (e.g. housing, environmental health and education) are, like the NHS, now locked into new financial management structures which have to control both their expenditure and activity. This surely makes working together across structural boundaries problematic, and in any case, there are no formal frameworks for sharing the cost of creating new programmes for health promotion. Whilst there are continuing downward pressures on public spending, other statutory programmes may well take precedence over any suggested ideas for health promotional activity coming from the Department of Health.

In a similar way, it could be argued that the attainment of targets expressed within the document is approached also with a lack of seriousness. For example, we might look to reduction in teenage smoking which is clearly linked to targets in reducing the incidence of coronary heart disease and lung cancer in the longer term. Sadly, a lack of progress in reducing teenage smoking is already being reported only a year after the publication of the strategy (Pilkington, 1993). Should we be surprised at the lack of progress? A persistent refusal to ban cigarette advertising by the Government, in spite of evidence to suggest that it does encourage young people to take up smoking, casts doubt upon the Government's commitment to health promotion. The Voluntary Code is certainly flouted by the tobacco industry, who continue to promote, as one would expect, the development of its own business. For example, the Health Education Authority have recently felt compelled to appeal for a ban on a specific set of advertisements, which over one year, has developed a cult appeal among young teenagers in Northern England and Scotland. Reg, the man in the advertisement, apparently appeals to the teenagers' irreverent attitude to authority, and the particular company he represents is doing excellent new business amongst the young (*Nursing Times*, 1993b). One wonders if this particular evidence might yet sway the Health Minister to take the proverbial U turn and listen to what many health professionals have been claiming for a long time: that tobacco advertising is bad news, and will continue to encourage young people to smoke.

If no change is made, then perhaps the cynical observer might begin to wonder if the Government has a vested interest in the growing success of the tobacco industry. Clearly, tax revenues from it are immense, and no government has refused these so far. Perhaps there are also Conservative MPs and Conservative Party supporters who have financial and other interests in maintaining the status quo for as long as possible.

Another bone of contention around this topic of teenage smoking is the appearance of apparently incompatible health policies. For example, if it is so important to promote healthy lifestyles amongst teenagers, why do we see the persistent decline in the numbers of school nurses and health visitors in employment (*Nursing Times*, 1993a). It does seem that this particular strategy is pretty hollow under examination. This is of no surprise, however; other targets have been examined and avenues needed to achieve some success followed through in a similar way – and the same sort of conclusions have been reached. The strategy appears long on words, but short on logical action.

Sadly, if this is the case, then the potentially exciting opportunities for nurses both to develop and to enrich their health promotion remit begin to look limited. The fact that the NHS reforms also point rather more towards an illness service for patients, would suggest that any expansion of activity into wider public health arenas and positive health approaches is looked to as a challenge for others outside the NHS to take up, rather than for those within.

Finally then we move to Chapter 5 in which we looked at the nursing profession, and how the reforms were apparently having an impact on both its development and future survival. The discussion considered the somewhat precarious standing of nursing as a profession over time, but also acknowledged the clear strides that have been made in recent years. It was suggested however that this, and previous Conservative Governments have sought to challenge and contain all professional power within the NHS, a move from which nurses have not been immune.

The imposition of General Management following the Griffiths' Inquiry (Griffiths, 1983) was suggested as the beginning of managerial control over the nursing profession. The present reforms were seen as continuing to tighten that control further. This has manifested itself in clinical directorates holding financial control of spending and activity, a clear support for non-registered health care assistants to carry out delegated caring tasks, a decrease in the number of registered nurses in employment, vacant qualified nurse posts left unfilled, an increasing development of skill–mixing in order to gain so-called 'value for money', and arguments made that trained nurses should be able and prepared to work in any place at any time as staffing levels require. None of this smacks of support for a developing profession, but rather the opposite. It reflects a clear denial of nurses autonomy and lacks any acknowledgement of the depth of knowledge or skill of the registered nurse.

Allied to these concerns is the fact that efforts made to maintain and uphold standards of nursing care have not been made easy in the post-reform era. The increasingly authoritarian nature of much NHS management has made it difficult to speak out about the negative impacts of the changes without a fear of reprisal. Nurses have faced a clear dilemma, because to ignore the Nurse Code of Conduct and to keep quiet on issues of concern is unprofessional, but to speak in defence of it may risk disciplinary action or even dismissal. If this is the case, then nursing's professional status is facing a very serious challenge which looks set to continue for the forseeable future.

It was suggested in the discussion that moves were afoot towards the creation of a small, élite professional nurse group, who were highly qualified, and would receive the power and financial remuneration commensurate with their acknowledged professional status. However, if this route was taken, it would leave the majority of nurses in some other non-professional, and thus less well paid category of employee. This possibility should be cause for some serious debate amongst nurses, and without a doubt has the potential for being extremely divisive in outcome. In the meantime, if nursing is to survive as a profession, then its members will have to act quickly, otherwise the die is likely to be cast in a way inconsistent with nurses' hopes and values.

What to do now?

The main thesis of this book has been that the changes taking place in the NHS are potentially detrimental to the provision of patient care, and to the professional scope of the role of the nurse. Implied has been a series of suggestions which can be acted upon at either a personal or a collective level, especially in so far as nurses have a individual professional and political interest in what happens in the NHS, and in what happens to patient care.

Some nurses may respond adversely to the notion of political involvement, arguing that this is contrary to professional ethics. At the same time, the same nurses may readily and enthusiastically accept that their professional responsibility to the patient and to the NHS will in turn necessitate involvement in discussion about the allocation and the use of resources: in fact, involvement is the very stuff of politics.

This is not the same as saying that as part of nurse professionalism it is desirable, perhaps even essential, to join one of the major political parties, and to try to use that party as a vehicle to further their own professional interests, and those of the patients. There would, in any case, be some difficulty in this strategy, as a substantial minority of nurses still vote Conservative, the party regarded by many other nurses as largely responsible for the woes of the NHS.

Whilst not denying the value of party political involvement, there is a danger that this becomes something of a static strategy. General Elections take place on average once every four years. Even if Labour were to promise at the next general election that they would replace the market-based reforms in the NHS, and that they would move towards a health system more consistent with nurses' professional values, there are still two obvious dangers: firstly, a possible process of waiting until the election campaign, and, thereby, becoming inactive in any intervening political controversy about the NHS and, secondly, a risk of putting all eggs in one basket, when there can never be a guarantee of an election result.

There is, though, an alternative, which would require nurses translating their professional commitment into, when necessary, public and collective argument, and campaigning for a health service which is adequately resourced, which treats patients according to clinical need rather than priorities determined by the dictates of the market or the bank balance, and which, in line with the aspirations of the service itself, takes due regard of the professionalism of nurses. Such an alternative will not be easy, management will not always like it, nurses themselves will often find difficult the transition of carer to debater and the collective organizations representing nurses, and competing for their support, will often send confused signals. Nevertheless, it is in the debate about the future organization of the NHS, about the allocation of resources for health issues, and about the role of the nurse in health care, that nurses collectively can shape their own future, and that of the NHS.

This book does not aim to set out a future prescriptive agenda for nurses. The purposes of this book have been different: to awaken interest, and to stimulate controversy. If those objectives have been achieved, involvement in a broader political debate about health care can follow with confidence. Which politician would then be foolish enough to resist the collective voice of nurses, as they argue for a better resourced and fairer NHS?

References

Blunkett David in Brindle D (1993) Hospital waiting lists 'top 1m for first time'. *The Guardian*, July 1.

Brindle David (1993a) Good news unit to write the NHS success story. *The Guardian*, May 17.

Brindle David (1993b) Health ads upset Labour. *The Guardian*, September 11.

Davies P (1993) Decline and fall. *Health Service Journal*, August 26.

Editorial (1993) Patients will lose patience. *Sunday Observer*, August 29.

Griffiths Roy (1983) *NHS Management Inquiry*. London.

Harrison J (1993) TUC is told how Tory policies blight health. *Nursing Times*, **89**(37).

Karmi G (1993) Ofhealth. *Health Service Journal*, July 29.

Mason P (1993) Market mayhem. *Nursing Times*, **89**(37).

Nursing Times (1993a) MPs demand more school nurse posts. **89**.

Nursing Times (1993b) HEA wants ad figure banned. **89**(40).

Pilkington Edward (1993) Health drive fails to stop one in ten children smoking. *The Guardian*, September 29.

Ross P in Brindle D (1993) Two-tier NHS breaks pledge. *The Guardian*, September 16.

Index